See Of

O9-BTM-376

DISCARD

R01087 19565

KF
4528.5
.M567
1994

Mitchell, Ralph.

CQ's guide to the
U.S. Constitution.

$18.95

DATE			

CHICAGO PUBLIC LIBRARY
ORIOLE PARK BRANCH
5201 N. OKETO   60656   BAKER & TAYLOR

CQ's Guide
TO THE
U.S. Constitution

Second Edition

Ralph Mitchell

CHICAGO PUBLIC LIBRARY
ORIOLE PARK BRANCH
5201 N. OKETO   60656

Congressional Quarterly Inc.
Washington, D.C.

To my family

to the Founders,
who activated the power in the People,

and to the People,
who must hold on to it.

Copyright © 1994 Congressional Quarterly Inc.
1414 22nd Street, N.W., Washington, D.C. 20037

All rights reserved. No part of this publication may be reproduced or transmitted in any form or by any means, electronic or mechanical, including photocopy, recording, or any information storage and retrieval system, without permission in writing from the publisher.

Printed in the United States of America

Cover: Ed Atkeson/Berg Design
Graphics: Kachergis Book Design
Typesetter: Jessica Forman

"The Constitutional Balance" and "Constitutional Amendments After Ratification of the Bill of Rights" courtesy of John Bibby, *Governing by Consent: An Introduction to American Politics,* 2nd ed., copyright © 1995 Congressional Quarterly Inc.

Library of Congress Cataloging-in-Publication Data
Mitchell, Ralph.
 CQ's guide to the U.S. Constitution / Ralph Mitchell. -- 2nd ed.
  p.   cm.
 ISBN 1-56802-010-6 (pbk.)
 1. United States--Constitutional law--Indexes.   I. Title.
KF4528.5.M567   1994
342.73'02--dc20
[347.3022]   94-49724
                                                           CIP

CHICAGO PUBLIC LIBRARY
ORIOLE PARK BRANCH
5201 N. OKETO   60656

R01087 19565

Conl

CHICAGO PUBLIC LIBRARY
HOWARD PARK BRANCH
3301 N. OKETO

Editors' Note

In this book, the editors of Congressional Quarterly have joined with Ralph Mitchell to provide a handy and easy to use reference on the Constitution of the United States. Mr. Mitchell, as he explains in his preface, has created an index that allows students and other persons to find their way quickly to the constitutional provision of interest to them. To this, Mr. Mitchell has added a glossary that will help readers understand the terms used. The editors of Congressional Quarterly have supplemented this basic material with a brief history of the writing of the Constitution in 1787. This material, drawn from other CQ publications, constitutes the first half of the book and helps the reader understand the roots of the document that has been the basic law of the United States for two centuries.

Preface

Early one morning a political discussion started among some of my fellow teachers at New Trier West High School, in Northfield, Illinois. At one point, just before the bell rang for classes, a need arose to look up some provision or other in the Constitution. Then the bell ended the discussion. I have forgotten the provision, but the fact that there had been a need to look it up stayed with me. After searching for a reference book on the subject, and finding none, I began to realize that such a need must arise many times, and that it would be a useful tool. The United States Constitution is a magnificent document, remarkably simple and direct when one considers the stature of the system which it, in the hands of the Founders, set in motion. But it would be too much to expect that it could deal with both the complexities of the system and the problem of making all of its provisions and concepts easily located by those who want to know. On the other hand, any detail of a democracy's most fundamental law should be readily accessible to the people. It is better that the Constitution is admired up close than from a distance. So it was my first purpose to compile an index to fill this need.

As work progressed, however, two additional benefits emerged naturally within the index structure. One was that all provisions related to a specific major element of our government system collected themselves under main index headings, such as "States," "Congress," "House of Representatives," and so on. These topics are dealt with in so many articles and sections that there is no other way to focus on them than with the aid of groupings of provisions under main headings.

A second benefit was the opportunity to include important features inherent in our system: checks and balances, the federal relationship between national and state governments, due process of law, and civil rights and liberties. Under such headings are listed the references necessary to see how each feature was created.

Finally, it was because of such terms as "bill of attainder," "compulsory process," and "letters of marque and reprisal" that I felt that a glossary of the Constitution's terminology would be of help in understanding it further. I hope that joining the two—index and glossary—will help make the supreme law of our land more familiar ground and less awesome to behold, but no less grand.

Ralph Mitchell

The Evolving Constitution

Constitutions, including that of the United States, are a special kind of law that set down basic rules for governments and the people who run them. A constitution grants powers—some of them explicitly spelled out and others implied or assumed—to public officials. A constitution also prohibits officials from conduct or actions that are considered harmful to citizens of a nation or a state. In addition, a constitution distributes powers between different parts of a government, often so that one part is not more powerful than any other. People who live in a nation or state with a constitution, whether they are citizens going about their daily business or individuals who choose to help run the government, live under what is called constitutional government.

A constitution, then, is a set of laws that people accept as fundamental and basic to the structure and operation of their government. The most successful constitutions are not long or overly detailed; rather, they set out the broad powers (and limitations on power) of public officials and leave the details to elected persons to complete. And because they are accepted as basic and long-lasting, the best constitutions are seldom changed and then only for the most convincing of reasons.

It might seem, as a result, that writing the Constitution of the United States would have been a fairly easy job. In fact, it was anything but easy. It was done by fifty-five men (no women participated) who met in Philadelphia in May 1787 to solve some problems experienced by the new nation that had emerged after winning its independence from Great Britain. In fact, the Philadelphia gathering, known as the Constitutional Convention, started with the modest goal of just "fixing" the existing form of government. Understanding what happened requires understanding what had been going on in the new country before then.

The people who lived in what was to become the United States of America did not, until around the 1770s, think of themselves as "Americans," but rather as English citizens who had come to live in a place away from England but still a part of that nation. These were the people of the colonies living in the New World. Their heritage was English and that heritage, so far as it pertained to governments, began centuries earlier. The development of the concept of constitutional government went back in England as early as 1215, when King John was forced by his most important subjects to sign a document known as the Magna Carta (the Great Charter). The Magna Carta put certain limits on the king's power, including his authority to raise royal revenue through taxation without the consent of a council of noblemen from throughout his realm.

This event is cited as one of the most important in the evolution to constitutional government; over the next several hundred years supreme power in England was gradually transferred from the monarch to the people, acting through representatives. The council King John faced was the forerunner of the British Parliament. During its evolution, the English obtained other rights that protected them against arbitrary and excessive exercise of power by the king. These traditions and expectations traveled with the people who moved to the New World and were incorporated into the governments of the thirteen original colonies. However, the colonies had no voice, no representatives, in Parliament.

The Seeds of Rebellion

The people living in the American colonies began to develop a greater national identity with the end of the French and Indian War in 1763. The war, part of a world conflict between the great powers of the day, particularly England and France, settled the destiny of Canada, which would become part of the British Em-

The Founding of a New Nation

1763

British defeat the French in North America in the French and Indian War.

1765

Britain imposes the Stamp Act on the colonies.

1773

Britain enacts the Tea Act, and colonists in Massachusetts stage the Boston Tea Party.

1774

First Continental Congress meets in Philadelphia and asserts that the British Parliament has no authority over the colonies internal affairs.

1775

Battles of Lexington and Concord.

1776

Second Continental Congress adopts the Declaration of Independence.

New state constitutions adopted between 1776 and 1784.

1777

Second Continental Congress adopts the Articles of Confederation.

1781

British surrender at Yorktown.

States complete ratification of the Articles of Confederation.

1786

Shays's Rebellion.

Annapolis Convention petitions the Continental Congress to call a constitutional convention.

1787

Constitutional Convention meets in Philadelphia and drafts the Constitution of the United States of America.

1787-1788

Eleven states ratify the Constitution, including the large states of New York and Virginia.

1789

First elections held under the Constitution.

The First Congress convenes, and George Washington is inaugurated the nation's first president.

North Carolina ratifies the Constitution.

1790

Rhode Island becomes the last of the thirteen original states to ratify the Constitution.

1791

Bill of Rights is ratified by the states.

Source: John Bibby, *Governing by Consent: An Introduction to American Politics,* 2nd ed. (Washington, D.C.: CQ Press, 1995), p. 34.

pire, and left England in control of virtually all the land east of the Mississippi River.

But the victory did not come cheap. It doubled the national debt of England and quadrupled the prospective cost of administering the greatly enlarged empire in America. The British expected the colonies to help pay the costs of the war as well as the increasing expenses of running the colonies. To do this, the British government began imposing various taxes and other laws on the colonies that were damaging to commercial activity and appeared to the colonists to violate the rights from their English heritage. Among the taxes and laws were these.

- A 1764 revenue act placing new duties on colonial imports such as wine, linen, and silk, and increasing the list of colonial goods that could be sold only to England.
- The Quartering Act of 1765 requiring colonies to help support the troops England would station in America, including supplying the troops with barracks or other quarters and with some of their provisions.
- The Stamp Act of 1765 imposing a tax on legal documents, newspapers, almanacs, and other items.

None of these measures sat well with the Americans, but the Stamp Act was particularly onerous because it was the first direct tax ever laid on the colonies by Parliament. Americans felt they could be taxed only by their own assemblies and that the Stamp Act, which was taxation without representation, violated their rights. The Stamp Act was repealed in 1766 when it became clear that it could not be enforced effectively in the face of increasingly hostile resistance from the colonies. But it was followed by other laws from Parliament in a similar vein that further poisoned the atmosphere.

Relations worsened in 1773 in an event now famous as the Boston Tea Party. England allowed the East India Company, a commercial undertaking, to dump a large quantity of surplus tea in the colonies, a move that threatened to harm American traders. Although many merchants favored simply boycotting these shipments, radicals urged more direct action. On December 16, 1773, a group disguised as Indians boarded three tea ships and dumped their cargoes into Boston Harbor. England struck back with a number of laws, which became known as the Intolerable Acts in the colonies. They included closing the Boston port until the cost of the lost tea was repaid, revising the charter that set up the Massachusetts colony to give England more control, and transferring to England the trials of royal officers charged with murder. In addition, another law gave to the French-Canadian—and Catholic—royal province of Quebec all of the land west of the Appalachians lying north of the Ohio River and east of the Mississippi, an act that alienated much of Protestant America. The Quebec Act of 1774 was seen as another punitive measure by most colonists and helped muster broad support for a "general congress of all the colonies" proposed by the Virginia and Massachusetts assemblies.

First Continental Congress

The call for a "general congress" was well received: only Georgia did not send delegates. The First Continental Congress met in Philadelphia on September 5, 1774. The Congress adopted a Declaration of Rights and Grievances against all British acts to which "Americans cannot submit" and approved commercial boycotts of many goods traded with England. The delegates adjourned in late October, agreeing to meet the following May if necessary. In England King George III declared the colonies were "now in a state of rebellion."

Events moved inexorably the following spring toward declaring independence, which led to war. Massachusetts was a center of the most vocal resistance to England. Rebels soon controlled all of the colony except Boston where the governor, Gen. Thomas Gage, was installed with five thousand troops.

On April 19, 1775, Gage sent one thousand of his soldiers to destroy the patriots' stores of ammunition in Lexington and Concord. They were met by Minutemen, and shooting broke out. British casualties were 247 dead and wounded before Gage's

The Constitutional Balance

Problems Confronting the Drafters of the Constitution	Constitutional Features Designed to Resolve the Problems

Creating a government based on the consent of the governed while avoiding the evils of factions and excesses of democracy	A government of divided powers
	• Separation of powers and checks and balances
	• Federalism (the constitutional division of governmental powers between the national government and the states)
	  • Bicameral legislature
	  • An appointed judiciary
	System of direct popular elections and indirect elections

Creating a government capable of governing while preventing that government from becoming too strong and a threat to individual liberties	Granting extensive powers to the national government while imposing constitutional limits on governmental authority Dividing powers to make it difficult for any group, faction, or temporary majority to gain control of government
Creating a union out of relatively independent states while preventing the creation of too powerful a national government and permitting state autonomy	Federal supremacy doctrine Federalism
Creating representative government while preventing the legislative excesses that characterized the post-Revolution period	Direct popular election of the House of Representatives, with indirect election of the Senate by the state legislatures Separation of powers to check the legislature Explicit limits on legislative power
Creating an executive strong enough to coordinate the operations of the government and check the legislature while preventing the executive from becoming an arbitrary ruler	Creating the office of president with specified powers Separation of powers to check executive power Election of the president for a fixed term; no hereditary executive

forces could get back to Boston. This encounter turned out to be the beginning of the Revolutionary War, although more than a year would pass before Americans were sufficiently united to declare their independence.

Second Continental Congress

When the Second Continental Congress met in Philadelphia on May 10, 1775, most delegates still hoped to avoid war with England. But faced with pleas for help from Massachusetts, the delegates agreed to raise an army and ask the colonies for funds to pay for it. George Washington, a delegate from Virginia, was made the Continental Army's commander in chief.

The delegates approved a petition to the king asking for a "happy and permanent reconciliation" between the colonies and England. Another declaration disavowed any desire for independence but resolved "to die free men rather than live slaves." The king was not pleased. In August he proclaimed a state of rebellion in the colonies, and England began hiring mercenaries in Germany and inciting the Iroquois Indians against the colonials.

Declaration of Independence

By the following summer, the Continental Congress was under increasing pressure from the most vocal radicals in the colonies to move to independence. In June 1776 a group of delegates was named to draft a declaration, but the actual writing fell largely to Thomas Jefferson. The Declaration of Independence, celebrated by Americans every year on July 4, was in large part a recitation of every grievance against English colonial policy that had emerged since 1763.

Its enduring quality, however, came from the Preamble as a statement of political philosophy with universal appeal.

> We hold these truths to be self-evident, that all men are created equal, that they are endowed by their Creator with certain

unalienable Rights, that among these are Life, Liberty, and the pursuit of Happiness. That to secure these rights, Governments are instituted among Men, deriving their just powers from the consent of the governed. That whenever any Form of Government becomes destructive of these ends it is the Right of the People to alter or to abolish it, and to institute new Government, laying its foundation on such principles and organizing its powers in such form, as to them shall seem most likely to effect their Safety and Happiness.

The Declaration of Independence committed the colonies to wage a war that was already under way and would drag on for more than five years before England gave up the struggle. *(For the full text of the Declaration, see p. 39.)*

New Colonial Governments

During the war provisional governments were set up in many colonies, patriots took control of provincial assemblies and conventions, and the royal governors and judges began to leave. A year after the signing of the Declaration of Independence, all but three of the colonies had written new constitutions and moved to establish new governments.

Although they varied in detail, all had similarities. All were written—Great Britain had no written constitution. All included or were accompanied by some kind of "Bill of Rights" to secure those English liberties that George III had violated, such as freedom of speech, press, and petition, and the rights of habeas corpus and trial by jury. All paid tribute to the idea of separation of powers between the legislative, executive, and judicial branches, although in every state the legislatures were far stronger than the executive. This reflected the colonists' fear of executive power that grew from their conflicts with the English Crown and the royal governors.

All the constitutions recognized the people as sovereign, but few entrusted them with much power. Most states adhered to pre-Revolutionary limits on suffrage. Ownership of some amount of property was generally required as a qualification to vote, and more usually was required to hold office.

These state constitutions became forerunners of the national Constitution that was to be created a little later. But before that could happen the colonies had to experience and test a different kind of organization for their new nation.

Articles of Confederation

The peace treaty was signed on September 3, 1783, exactly twenty years after the end of the French and Indian War. Once free of England, the colonies were little more than a handful of small—although growing—collections of pioneers facing serious challenges in a frontier land. At the same time in June 1776 that prominent patriots were calling for a Declaration of Independence, several also urged the drafting a plan of confederation that would be sent to the colonies for consideration.

A plan was prepared by July 12, but it was not until more than a year later, November 15, 1777, that the Continental Congress adopted the Articles of Confederation and Perpetual Union. And it was not until five years later that enough of the states voted their approval for the Articles to go into effect.

The Articles reflected the dominant motive of Americans who were rebelling against British rule: to preserve their freedoms from the encroachments of centralized power. A strong federal government with wide powers was never an option. There was less agreement on other matters. Significant tensions developed over the relative standing of the thirteen states in the confederation. A central issue was whether the more populous states would have a larger say in the national government, an issue that was to remain vexing during drafting of the United States Constitution a few years later.

In the new government, there was no president and no court. Congress remained the sole organ of government; the states retained their equality, each having one vote; and of the specific powers delegated to Congress, the most important could not be exercised without the agreement of nine of the thirteen states. Moreover, Congress had no power to tax. The states were to provide funds to pay the costs, but Congress was not given the power to compel compliance. Amendments to the original Articles required unanimous approval of the states. One of the most serious weaknesses was the absence of power by the national government to regulate commerce among the states and with foreign nations.

These problems were compounded by major difficulties in the states following the Revolutionary War that threatened economic and political stability. Congress was powerless to resolve a postwar conflict between creditors and debtors that was aggravated by an economic depression and a shortage of currency. Most states had stopped issuing paper money and tried to pay off their war debts by raising taxes. In addition, merchants and other creditors began to demand that debtors repay private debts. Pressed on all sides, the debtors (mostly farmers) clamored for relief through state laws to put off the collection of debts and to provide cheap money.

In response, a number of states started issuing paper money again, but in Massachusetts, where the commercial class held power, the state refused and passed a program of high taxes. Cattle and land were seized for debts, debtors crowded the jails, and all petitions for relief were ignored.

Out of this came Shays's Rebellion of 1786, an uprising of distressed farmers in central Massachusetts led by Daniel Shays. Although the rebellion was put down quickly by the state militia, there was much sympathy for the rebels. Their leaders were treated leniently, and a newly elected legislature acted to meet some of their demands. More important, the rebellion aroused the fear of many Americans for the future, and in particular frightened the powerful commercial class of citizens who saw a looming threat to their wealth if economic issues were not resolved. Congress had been unable to give Massachusetts any help—further evidence of the weakness of the Confederation. Everyone was heading down a road toward a new government.

Madison on the Constitution

"If men were angels, no government would be necessary. If angels were to govern men, neither external nor internal controls on government would be necessary. In framing a government which is to be administered by men over men, the great difficulty lies in this: you must first enable the government to control the governed; and in the next place oblige it to control itself. A dependence on the people is, no doubt, the primary control on the government; but experience has taught mankind the necessity of auxiliary precautions."

—James Madison, *The Federalist*, No. 51

The state of the Union under the Articles of Confederation was a source of growing concern to leading Americans well before Shays's Rebellion shook the confidence of a wider public. In extensive correspondence as early as 1780, George Washington, John Jay, Thomas Jefferson, James Madison, James Monroe, and others expressed their fears that the Union could not survive the strains of internal dissension and external weakness without some strengthening of central authority.

How to achieve that goal was not yet clear. Opinions varied widely as to what type of new government would have sufficient power to meet the needs of a growing nation.

At Hamilton's urging the New York Assembly asked Congress in 1782 to call a general convention of the states to revise the Articles. Congress studied the proposal but did not reach any agreement. Then, Virginia and Maryland in 1785 worked out a plan to resolve conflicts between themselves over navigation and commercial regulations. Their agreement gave Madison the idea of calling a general meeting to solve commercial problems. In January 1786 the Virginia Assembly issued the call for a meeting in Annapolis in September.

Nine states named delegates to the Annapolis convention, but the dozen persons who assembled represented only five states.

Rather than seek a commercial agreement from so small a group, Madison and Hamilton persuaded the delegates on September 14 to adopt a report that described the state of the Union as "delicate and critical." The report recommended that the states appoint commissioners to meet the next May in Philadelphia "to devise such further provisions as shall appear to them necessary to render the constitution of the Federal Government adequate to the exigencies of the Union."

The proposal was deliberately vague because its backers knew there was still strong opposition in the colonies to giving the central government much more power. The Virginia Assembly, prodded by Madison and Washington, agreed in October to send delegates, and six other states took similar action. Congress the following February moved to retain control of the situation by passing a resolution endorsing the proposed convention for the purpose of reporting to it. Officially, therefore, the convention was to be no more than advisory to Congress.

That is not what happened. Soon after the Philadelphia convention opened, the delegates were asked to decide whether to try to patch up the Articles of Confederation or to ignore them and draw up a new plan of government. Congress, the state legislatures, and many of the delegates expected the session in Philadelphia to do no more than draft proposals to revise the Articles in ways that would somehow strengthen the Confederation without altering the system of state sovereignty. But Madison and others who had worked to bring about the convention were convinced of the need for fundamental reform.

Writing the Constitution

The task began at the State House in Philadelphia May 25, 1787. George Washington was unanimously chosen president of the convention. In four months the delegates drafted a document known to the world today as the Constitution of the United States. But it did not come easily. Over a sweltering summer, the delegates debated fundamental principles of government organization. Out of this debate, in which the conflicts at times were so intense it was feared the convention itself would collapse, came a radical new form of government unknown to the world and which no person of the times would have thought possible even a decade earlier.

The Delegates

The convention was controversial from the beginning, with some Revolutionary leaders, fearful that the meeting would centralize power in the new nation, refusing to attend. Rhode Island did not even send delegates. Only fifty-five of the seventy-four delegates to the convention actually attended. But they were a distinguished group, spoken of today as the single greatest collection of political thinkers ever assembled. Virtually all were experienced in government: seven former governors, thirty-nine former members of the Continental Congress, and a number of others who helped write state constitutions only a few years earlier. They were mostly men of wealth and status, and they were relatively young, with an average age of forty-two. The most prominent were James Madison of Virginia, who had drafted that state's constitution; Alexander Hamilton of New York, the most outspoken advocate of a strong and far-reaching national government; George Washington of Virginia, whose prestige from the Revolutionary era was essential to the convention's credibility; Benjamin Franklin of Pennsylvania, the senior statesman of the times, whose experience and personal charm helped bring factions together (and at eighty-one the oldest delegate); James Wilson of Pennsylvania, who contributed much to the Constitution's articles on the presidency and executive branch; and Gouverneur Morris, also of Pennsylvania, who headed the committee on style that drafted much of the document's final language. One central figure of the times, Thomas Jefferson, was not there; he was in Europe serving as a diplomat.

The thinking of these men was shaped not only by their experience with the power of the British Crown but also by philosophers such as John Locke who believed in a natural law that entitled every person to life, liberty, and property, and that the role of government was to protect these rights. They were also the product of other strains of seventeenth-century thinking that distrusted human nature, which they believed was essentially self-serving and needed to be restrained. They had little faith in popular rule, but they also believed in popular sovereignty that made the people—not a king or any other authority figure or set of beliefs—the source of government authority.

Creating a new government that acknowledged and balanced these sometimes inconsistent beliefs between popular sovereignty and a human tendency toward destructive self-interest was a major challenge. The Constitution they wrote, and the government that was created under it, has proven a remarkable mixture of powers and limits on power that has survived and adapted to changing times for more than two centuries.

Virginia and New Jersey Plans

The convention delegates reached agreement on numerous issues with little difficulty. Within a week they agreed that the new government should have three parts—a national legislature, an executive, and a judiciary—and that the government's powers would be greater than those given under the Articles of Confederation. They accepted the principle of an elected legislature that would be bicameral—consisting of two chambers—and the executive would be one person who was elected (although initially it was thought that election would be by the state legislatures rather than the people generally).

Much of this structure was included in the Virginia Plan, a package of resolutions put forth by the advocates of a strong central government that would be unitary. That is, it would operate directly on the people and be independent of the states. It was to be a "national government" in contrast to the "merely federal" system that existed under the Articles and was found inadequate. Many understood a national government to mean a regime of potentially unlimited powers that would extinguish the independence of the states. Although the backers of the Virginia Plan wanted a strong central authority, they were proposing to create a system in which national and state governments would exercise dual sovereignty over the people within separate and prescribed fields. Such a dual system, unknown in 1787, was later recognized as one of the most remarkable creations of the Founders.

The biggest problem, however, arose from the Virginia Plan's provisions that both chambers of the national legislature be based on population. The smaller states saw this provision as a guarantee of domination by the most populous states, Virginia, Pennsylvania, New York, and Massachusetts. The small states responded with the New Jersey Plan, which retained the single chamber (unicameral) legislature that was in use under the Articles of Confederation. Other provisions also made the new government much more of a federal system than the nationalists thought necessary.

The delegates voted for the principle advocated by the nationalists: a new and more powerful central government that replaced, rather than merely reworked, the government of the Confederation. The big state/small state dispute was settled by the Connecticut compromise, also called the Great Compromise. This scheme called for a two-chamber national legislature. The House of Representatives would be based on population and elected by the people, and the Senate would have two members from each state who were elected by state legislatures.

Structure and Power of Government

There was little if any dispute in the Philadelphia convention that the new national government should consist of three branches—legislative, executive, and judicial—and this in turn implied broad acceptance of the principle of separation of powers.

Congress

The Virginia Plan provided for two houses of the national legislature, as was the practice in the English Parliament and in most of the colonial governments and ten of the thirteen states. Thus, the two-house practice was well known in America, even though it was not used in either the Continental Congress or the Congress of the Articles of Confederation, which were unicameral.

The Constitutional Convention continued to speak of the "Legislature of the United States" and its "first branch" and "second branch" until those terms were changed in early August 1787 to the terms used today: Congress, the House of Representatives, and the Senate. The term *Congress* was taken from the Articles of Confederation, and the other terms were widely used in the state legislatures.

For the House, the delegates accepted the premise of the nationalists that the new government rest on the consent of the people rather than on the state legislatures. Delegates fearful of popular democracy argued for the latter, but their proposal was defeated twice in favor of a popular election for members of the House.

The Virginia Plan proposed that the House elect members to the Senate from persons nominated by the state legislatures, but this idea drew little support because it made the Senate subservient to the House. Instead, the delegates decided in June that state legislatures would elect their state's members to the Senate. This decision stood until 1913 when the Constitution was amended to provide for selection of senators by direct popular election.

The basis of representation also was a controversial matter, which was rooted in the slavery issue. The convention accepted the basic premise that representation in the House would be based on population, although the Virginia Plan provided for representation in proportion to a state's wealth or free population. The South wanted slaves to be counted for purpose of determining the number of seats given to each state in the House, but not counted in apportioning direct taxes (taxes paid directly to the government by individual citizens) among the states. Northern state delegates believed just the opposite. The result was the Three-fifths Compromise under which a slave was counted as three-fifths of a person for both purposes. The concept of wealth in deciding representation was dropped.

The issue of the size of Congress led to decisions on a national census. Early in July the delegates considered a proposal that each state have one vote in the House for every forty thousand inhabitants, a number later lowered to thirty thousand. Congress was given authority to regulate the future size of the House to allow for population growth and the admission of new states. But to prevent an existing majority from blocking apportionment changes, the delegates decided to link the apportionment of representatives to an "enumeration"—that is, a census—every ten years of the "whole number of free persons . . . and three fifths of all others." House membership was set at sixty-five until the first census. The Senate was fixed at two members per state.

Terms of office were set at two years for House members and six for senators, with one-third of that membership turning over every two years. Qualification for office was set at a minimum age of thirty for senators and twenty-five for representatives. The individual had to be a United States citizen (for seven years for the House and nine for the Senate) and "an Inhabitant" of the state to be represented when selected.

Powers of Congress

The advocates of a strong national government, such as Hamilton and Madison, came to the convention with the expectation of creating a fundamentally new institution that would remedy the shortcomings of the Articles of Confederation. High on the agenda were the powers that the new government would possess, with a particular focus on the legislative branch—Congress—that was at the center of the thinking and experience of the delegates.

The nationalists with their Virginia Plan came prepared with a broad grant of power. This language, which was quite general and sweeping, was debated carefully over the summer until the delegates settled on a list of enumerated powers for Congress. The delegates also included a list of powers to be denied to Congress and to the states. All of these eventually became part of Article I of the Constitution (Sections 8, 9, and 10). Following are the major provisions found in those sections:

Power to Tax. The delegates agreed without much dispute that Congress needed the power to tax to support the new government. The final language provided that Congress "shall have power to lay and collect taxes, duties, imposts and excises, to pay the debts and provide for the common defense and general welfare of the United States." The inclusion of the words "general welfare" has played an important role in subsequent debate, particularly in the modern period, about the purpose of the Founders. Advocates of proactive government have claimed this was a clear grant of additional and unspecified powers. Proponents of limited government argue that it was merely to clarify that taxation was not just for public debt repayment, but could not be taken as a creating authority beyond those specifically listed in the Constitution.

Delegates had to resolve which chamber—the Senate or House, or both—had authority over bills that raised revenue (taxes) or spent money (appropriations). The sentiment for some time was that this authority should rest with the House, which was common in the states, and not be changed by the Senate, even though a few states did allow that. The final language gave the House sole authority to originate tax bills but allowed the Senate to amend them. The distinction was not explicitly extended to cover appropriation bills. Nevertheless, the House over the years assumed, based on the debate in the convention, that it had the sole power to originate spending legislation, and this prerogative rests with the House to the present day.

Power to Regulate Commerce. Trade among the states and with other countries was severely handicapped under the Confederation by a lack of uniformity in duties and commercial regulation. States often discriminated against products of other states. The delegates were eager to remedy the problems, but regional conflict stood in the way. It was clear that southern states would not accept a constitution that did not protect their vested interest in slave labor and agricultural exports from possible burdensome restrictions that a Congress controlled by northerners might impose.

As a result, the convention included language giving Congress the power to regulate commerce with foreign nations and among the states but with two limitations: a ban on taxing exports and a prohibition on efforts to tax or outlaw the slave trade. The latter was particularly controversial and was modified to last for twenty years rather than indefinitely. In addition, Congress was allowed to levy a duty on slaves, as on other imports, up to $10 a person.

War and Treaty Power. The Articles of Confederation gave Congress the exclusive right and power of deciding issues of peace and war. The delegates proposed giving Congress as a whole the power to make war and the Senate alone the power to approve treaties. The latter was later changed to divide the power between the Senate and the president. The issue of war was more difficult. Some delegates thought the war power should be only with the president, while others favored giving it to the Senate. When neither prevailed, the delegates adopted language to give Congress the power "to declare war." The word "declare" had been substituted for "make" in order to leave the president free to repel a sudden attack. But in the twentieth century this issue became highly controversial as some presidents used other authority they believed they had to commit the nation to wars even though Congress had not declared war. Congress has passed legislation on the power to make war, but the issue has never been fully resolved.

Impeachment. Early in the convention delegates agreed that the president should be removable on impeachment (accusation) and conviction "of malpractice or neglect of duty." How this was to be done depended on who would select the president. At first Congress was to select the president, which made delegates leery of also allowing Congress to remove him. When choosing the president in normal circumstances was given to electors selected in the states (the electoral college), the delegates came up with the formula: impeachment by the House and trial and conviction by a two-thirds majority in the Senate. The causes for impeachment and removal would be "treason, bribery, or other high crimes and misdemeanors." Delegates also extended the impeachment provision to the vice president and other civil officers.

Express and Implied Powers. The delegates wrote into the Constitution many specific powers in addition to those most important ones already noted, including coining money, establishing a military, setting up post offices, and creating lower federal courts. Such powers are known as delegated, or express, powers.

But the Constitution and a very important early ruling by the Supreme Court added greatly to these powers. The delegates provided, in Article I, that "the Congress shall have the Power . . . to make all Laws which shall be necessary and proper for carrying into Execution the foregoing Powers, and all other Powers vested in this Constitution in the Government of the United States." This has come to be called the Necessary and Proper Clause or the Elastic Clause.

The conflicts evident during the drafting of the Constitution continued in the years after it was ratified. Advocates of a strong national government wanted to read these powers broadly, and supporters of a limited government favored rights of the states. They became known, respectively, as Federalists and Antifederalists and became the centers of political activity in the early years of the nation.

The Supreme Court's influence on this debate came in one of its most important early decisions, made in 1819, in a case called *McCulloch v. Maryland* in which the justices supported the cause of the Federalists. The case involved the United States Bank, created by Congress. Maryland said no such power existed in the Constitution and urged a strict interpretation of the document. In the decision by Chief Justice John Marshall, a staunch Federalist, the Court said it was reasonable that Congress would consider it "necessary and proper" to charter a national bank to carry out its various delegated fiscal powers. With that argument, Marshall created the doctrine of implied powers, allowing the government powers that can be reasonably implied from its delegated powers. Over the decades that followed, the *McCulloch* decision was the legal underpinning for extensions of powers in the national government, which reached their heights with the New Deal in the 1930s when the nation was in the depths of the Great Depression. Virtually all of modern legislation dealing with subjects the Founders never dreamed of—farm supports, housing subsidies, crime control, and thousands more—is rooted in the implied power doctrine from the earliest days.

In addition to express and implied powers, the government also operates under the doctrine, mainly in foreign affairs, of inherent powers, which usually is defined to mean powers not dependent directly on constitutional grants of authority but from the actual existence of the government. Examples include authority to occupy territory, make treaties, and conduct foreign relations. The Court has said these powers would exist regardless of the Constitution's wording or absence of wording on the subject because they are powers all national governments possess under international law.

Executive Branch and the President

The issue of the powers and structure of the executive created great difficulty in the convention because there was little in the nation's short life to use as a model. The office did not exist under the Articles of Confederation, which placed the executive function in Congress. In addition, the delegates and their contemporaries feared executive authority because of their long battle with the English Crown and its royal delegates in the colonies.

Qualifications, Election. The convention delegates decided to apply simple qualifications for a person holding the office, much as they had done for those serving in Congress. A president had to be thirty-five years of age, a natural-born citizen, and an inhabitant of the United States for fourteen years. The same qualifications were applied to the vice president.

The method of election and the term of office of the executive were closely related issues. If Congress were to choose the president, most delegates thought he should have a long term and be ineligible for reappointment. But if another selection method were used, then a shorter term and reeligibility was seen as the better arrangement. Thus the method of election became crucial.

Different approaches were considered. One scheme was to have the people choose the electors, who then would choose the president. The aristocrats at the convention, uneasy about popular democracy, thought—in the words of one—the people "too little informed of personal characters" to choose electors. Later, however, this idea gained support among the delegates and was finally approved in modified form that had the electors selected by the states with each state having the same number of electors as it had senators and representatives. The person receiving the majority of the electoral votes would become president and the one with the next largest vote vice president. The last part was changed by constitutional amendment in 1804 to prevent the election of a president from one party and a vice president from another. The plan also provided for a four-year term with no restriction as to reelection. The limit on reelection also was changed by constitutional amendment, in 1951, to limit a person to two terms.

Presidential Powers. Initially, the convention conferred only three powers on the president; "to carry into effect the National laws," to appoint to offices in cases not otherwise provided for, and to veto bills. Additional powers were added, mostly taken from state constitutions, including a directive to report "on the State of the Union" from time to time and to recommend legislation, making the president head of the army and navy, to convene and adjourn Congress under certain circumstances, and to see "that the Laws be faithfully executed."

The power to appoint also prompted much debate with many delegates wanting at least some of this authority vested in Congress. But by September the delegates approved giving the president power to appoint ambassadors and other public ministers, justices of the Supreme Court, and all other officers of the United States "by and with the consent of the Senate." With further modifications, these powers were approved.

Many delegates wanted the power to make treaties to be only in the Senate but that drew opposition. Madison urged giving the power to the president, representing the whole people. This idea won support but was qualified by the requirement that treaties be subject to the advice and consent of two-thirds of senators present on a vote.

The Judiciary

Article III of the Constitution, relating to "the judicial power of the United States," was developed in the Constitution with relative ease. The Virginia Plan called for "one or more supreme tribunals" and inferior tribunals (lower courts) to be appointed by the national legislature to try all cases involving crimes at sea, foreigners and citizens of different states, "collection of the national revenue," impeachments, and "questions which may involve the national peace and harmony." The convention went on to spell out the jurisdiction of these courts in greater detail, but the only basic changes made in the plan were to vest initially in the Senate and then in the presidency the power to appoint judges, and to transfer the trial of impeachments from the Supreme Court to the Senate.

Article III did not explicitly authorize the Court to pass on the constitutionality of acts of Congress, but the convention clearly anticipated the exercise of that power as one of the acknowledged functions of the courts. Several delegates noted that the state courts had "set aside" laws in conflict with the state constitutions. The convention debated at great length, and rejected four times, a proposal to link the Court with the president in the veto power.

One delegate favored it because "laws may be unjust, may be unwise, may be dangerous, may be destructive, and yet may not be so unconstitutional as to justify the judges in refusing to give them effect." Another agreed that the Court "could declare an unconstitutional law void." This power was given reality by Supreme Court decisions, beginning with the landmark case *Marbury v. Madison* in 1803.

The role of the judiciary in determining the constitutionality of the laws of the land also was implicit in the provision, incorporated in Article IV, that asserted that the Constitution, the laws, and the treaties of the United States "shall be the supreme Law of the Land." The Supremacy Clause was reinforced by a further provision in Article IV stating that all members of Congress and of the state legislatures, as well as all executive and judicial officers of the national and state governments, "shall be bound by Oath or Affirmation to support this Constitution."

Amending the Constitution

The Founders agreed on the need for an effective method to amend the Constitution. A major reason for calling the Constitutional Convention had been that the method for amending the Articles of Confederation—requiring unanimous consent of the states—had proved impractical. But the delegates also wanted to strike a balance between preserving their carefully crafted document with the need to alter the provisions under compelling circumstances.

Delegates at first supported a proposal that two-thirds of the states have the sole power to initiate amendments by petitioning Congress to call a convention. Later, near the end of the convention, Article V was altered to allow Congress to propose amendments—the only method that has been used in more than two hundred years—and requiring that Congress "shall" call a convention for the purpose of proposing amendments when requested to do so by two-thirds of the states. The latter approach, although never used, has always frightened advocates of a stable

Constitution that is difficult to change; they are concerned that a runaway convention prompted by the states could make far-reaching changes in the document. But in either case, the delegates agreed amendments would take effect when approved by three-fourths of the states.

Ratification

The delegates who met in the Constitutional Convention in 1787 went far beyond the purpose for which the gathering had been called, which was simply to revise the Articles of Confederation. Instead, they discarded that system of government and created a new one patterned on their experience in the states and the Confederation but unlike anything previously known. It was a product, and a victory, of the nationalists who were determined to provide the young United States with a strong national government that could deal, they believed, with the challenges that the Confederation was powerless to handle. They were not about to let their work be scuttled in the state legislatures, which they feared were hostile to the new Constitution.

The advocates of the Constitution, who became known as Federalists, set out aggressively to sell their document. The first step was to be sure that approval was not left to the state legislatures. They insisted that the Constitution be considered by "the supreme authority of the people themselves," as Madison put it. The Federalists wanted special conventions elected for the purpose of ratifying the new Constitution. Conventions would be more representative than the legislatures, they contended, because the legislatures would lose significant power under the new document. Accordingly, the Philadelphia convention provided that the Constitution should be submitted to popularly elected state conventions. The delegates also decided that the new Constitution would go into effect when approved by the conventions of nine of the thirteen states.

The convention adjourned on September 17, 1787. The Congress of the Confederation submitted the Constitution to the

The First Ten Amendments to the Constitution: The Bill of Rights

Amendment	Purpose
I	Guarantees freedom of religion, speech, assembly, and press, and the right of people to petition the government for redress of grievances
II	Protects the right of states to maintain a militia
III	Restricts quartering of troops in private homes
IV	Protects against "unreasonable searches and seizures"
V	Assures the right not to be deprived of "life, liberty, or property, without due process of law," including protections against double jeopardy, self-incrimination, and government seizure of property without just compensation
VI	Guarantees the right to a speedy and public trial by an impartial jury
VII	Assures the right to a jury trial in cases involving the common law (judge-made law originating in England)
VIII	Protects against excessive bail or cruel and unusual punishment
IX	Provides that people's rights are not restricted to those specified in Amendments I-VIII
X	Reiterates the Constitution's principle of federalism by providing that powers not granted to the national government nor prohibited to the states are reserved to the states and to the people

Source: John Bibby, *Governing by Consent: An Introduction to American Politics,* 2nd ed. (Washington, D.C.: CQ Press, 1995), p. 53.

states for consideration ten days later, starting the process that was to last until the following summer for formal ratification and until 1790 for ratification by the last of the original thirteen states.

During this period an intense and often bitter—and sometimes violent—battle was waged between the Federalists and the Antifederalists, who opposed ratification. The divisions between these groups had been developing for years but were given focus by the issue of creating a new government under a new Constitution. Although there were numerous exceptions, the division tended to reflect long-standing differences among Americans between commercial and agrarian interests, creditors and debtors, men of great or little property, tidewater planters and the small farmers of the interior.

Two historical events accompanied the ratification process. One was the drafting of the Bill of Rights—a bulwark of protection for the rights of Americans. The other was publication of a series of essays by supporters of ratification called *The Federalist.*

The absence of a bill of rights in the Constitution was a major sore point for many people, particularly the Antifederalists who feared that a powerful national government would infringe and perhaps even extinguish the individual freedoms of Americans who had struggled so hard to win in the revolution against England. Federalists did not consider this an issue because, they claimed, the national government would be limited to exercising the powers granted to it under the Constitution. Nevertheless, they did not vigorously argue the point and agreed to incorporate a bill of rights as the first amendments to the document following ratification.

These ten amendments were written to protect some of the most fundamental freedoms enjoyed by the people of the new nation, including freedom of speech, press, and religion; freedom from "unreasonable" searches and seizures by the government; the right to a speedy and public trial; and the right not to be deprived of "life, liberty, or property, without due process of law." All of these protections were aimed at the new national government, but over the decades that followed the Supreme Court slowly but steadily made some (but not all) of them applicable, through a process called incorporation, to state governments as well. The Bill of Rights was ratified on December 15, 1791.

In the meantime, however, the battle raged in the states over ratification of the Constitution itself. All of the newspapers of the day published extensive correspondence on the virtues and vices of the new plan of government. The fullest and strongest case for the Constitution was presented in a series of letters written by Madison, Hamilton, and John Jay under the pen name "Publius." Seventy-seven of the letters were published in New York City newspapers between October 27, 1787, and April 4, 1788, and in book form, along with eight additional letters, as *The Federalist* on May 28, 1788. These letters probably had only a small influence on ratification, but *The Federalist* came to be regarded as the classic exposition of the Constitution as well as one of the most important works on political theory ever written.

The Delaware convention on December 7, 1787, unanimously ratified the Constitution, the first state to do so. Pennsylvania came next, on December 12. (As an example of the heightened feelings of the day, Pennsylvania Federalists earlier had tried to move to call a convention for ratification before the new document had even been officially submitted to the states. On that move, nineteen Antifederalists withdrew from the Pennsylvania Assembly, depriving it of a quorum to act, until a mob seized two of them and dragged them back.) Following Pennsylvania other states fell into line until New Hampshire, on June 21, 1788, became the ninth state to ratify. This met the requirement for approval by nine states, but it was clear that without Virginia and New York the Constitution would stand on shaky ground. On June 25, in a vigorous battle led by Madison, Virginia ratified the document 89-79. New York ratified on July 26 by an even narrower margin, 30-27, after Hamilton and Jay threatened that without approval New York City would secede and join the Union as a separate state. The other two states of the original thirteen, North Carolina and Rhode Island, ratified in November 1789 and May 1790, respectively.

The government was on its way. The Congress of the Confederation, in accordance with the request of the Constitutional Convention, on September 13, 1788, designated New York City as the capital. It selected the first Wednesday of January 1789 as the day for choosing presidential electors, the first Wednesday of Febru-

The Struggle for Ratification of the Constitution

While most of the smaller states overwhelmingly supported ratification of the Constitution (New Hampshire and Rhode Island were exceptions), strong opposition existed in the larger states whose approval was crucial for the new government's success.

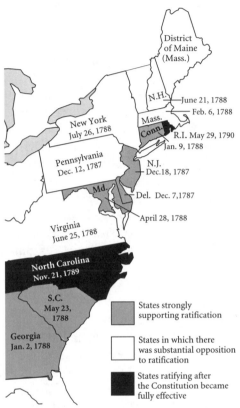

Pennsylvania. Ratification was gained over stubborn opposition by a vote of 46-23 and was accompanied by a demand for a bill of rights.

Massachusetts. When the state included a demand for a bill of rights with ratification, the initial skepticism of John Hancock and Samuel Adams was overcome.

Virginia. The opposition led by George Mason and Patrick Henry was overcome by an 89-79 vote on the understanding that amendments would be added later to the Constitution.

New York. Backed by arguments in *The Federalist,* Alexander Hamilton led the fight for ratification, which was won by a narrow 30-27 vote.

Source: John Bibby, *Governing by Consent: An Introduction to American Politics,* 2nd ed. (Washington, D.C.: CQ Press, 1995), p. 53.

ary for the meeting of electors, and the first Wednesday of March for the opening session of the first Congress under the new Constitution.

The Evolving Constitution

The work produced by the Founders more than two hundred years ago has remained remarkably stable. The Constitution had been amended only twenty-seven times as of the end of 1994, and many proposed amendments have fallen by the wayside. The heirs of the Founders have taken seriously the belief that a constitution should be a basic document, not overly long, enunciating simple but lasting principles that can adapt to changing circumstances. Many state constitutions go in the other direction, running to tens of thousands of words (the average is about 27,000 words compared to about 8,700 in the U.S. Constitution) that often are amended hundreds of times. These constitutions have more the flavor of statutory law—important, but tied to the times and easily changed.

But the U.S. Constitution is not unchanging. As previously noted, the Bill of Rights, which has played so important a role in protecting basic liberties, was added immediately as the first ten amendments as part of the effort to obtain ratification of the new Constitution. Later amendments abolished slavery, granted citizenship to all persons born or naturalized in the United States, authorized the income tax, limited presidents to two terms of office, guaranteed voting rights for all Americans (both for women, who had been denied the franchise into the twentieth century, and for blacks, who had been denied the franchise in many areas, particularly the South), provided for direct election of senators, and made other important changes.

Most of the amendments have been about fundamental rights of Americans on which there was considerable agreement or that addressed matters of the highest importance. Many other proposed amendments, particularly those that concern social or cultural matters that inflame factions at certain times, have been

Constitutional Amendments After Ratification
of the Bill of Rights

Amendments	Date	Purpose
Amendments Changing the Powers of the National and State Governments		
XI	1795	Removed cases in which a state was sued without its consent from the jurisdiction of the federal courts
XIII	1865	Abolished slavery and authorized Congress to pass legislation implementing its abolition
XIV	1868	Granted citizenship to all persons born or naturalized in the United States; banned states from denying any person life, liberty, or property without due process of law; and banned states from denying any person the equal protection of the laws
XVI	1913	Empowered Congress to levy an income tax
XVIII	1919	Authorized Congress to prohibit the manufacture, sale, and transportation of liquor
XXI	1933	Repealed the Eighteenth Amendment and empowered Congress to regulate the liquor industry
Amendments Changing Government Structure		
XII	1804	Required presidential electors to vote separately for president and vice president
XX	1933	Shortened the time between a presidential election and inauguration by designating January 10 as Inauguration Day; set January 3 as the date for the opening of a new Congress
XXII	1951	Limited presidents to two full terms in office
XXV	1967	Provided for succession to the office of president in the event of death or incapacity and for filling vacancies in the office of the vice president
XXVII	1992	Banned Congress from increasing its members' salaries until after the next election
Amendments Extending the Suffrage and Power of the Voters		
XV	1870	Extended voting rights to blacks by outlawing denial of the right to vote on the basis of race, color, or previous condition of servitude
XVII	1913	Provided for the election of U.S. senators by direct popular vote instead of by the state legislatures
XIX	1920	Extended the right to vote to women
XXIII	1961	Granted voters in the District of Columbia the right to vote for president and vice president
XXIV	1964	Forbade requiring the payment of a poll tax to vote in a federal election
XXVI	1971	Extended the right to vote to eighteen-year-olds

sidetracked before being added to the Constitution. One was not: prohibition. The Eighteenth Amendment authorized Congress to prohibit the manufacture, sale, and transportation of liquor. It was approved in 1919, but repealed in 1933 after little more than a decade of failed efforts to control distribution and consumption of liquor. Although by no means the only part of the Constitution repealed, prohibition is perhaps the most conspicuous as a failed experiment to use the Constitution to alter personal conduct.

The Changing Constitution

Formal amendment of the Constitution is the method of changing the document that is generally accepted as most desirable because it reflects the considered judgment by a wide array of popularly elected officials: Congress by a two-thirds vote recommends an amendment, which three-fourths of the state legislatures must approve before it becomes part of the Constitution. Another way to amend the Constitution is for the states to get Congress to call a convention to write amendments, but this method has never been used.

It is—by deliberate choice of the Founders—a slow and cumbersome process that protects against impetuous changes. The far more common way in which the Constitution changes is in interpretation of the provisions, which does not change the actual wording but rather the meaning of the words and their application to new situations. This process gives the Constitution new meaning to address contemporary (and changing) circumstances. Interpretation by courts, particularly the Supreme Court, is the best known part of the process, but all of the branches of government play an important role.

Congressional Interpretation. When Congress passes a law it is making an interpretation of the Constitution under the powers granted to it. The ability to interpret the Constitution allows Congress to make laws that affect everyone in areas that are not mentioned in the Constitution and in fact were never even known to the Founders. A common example in modern times is the Commerce Clause, which grants Congress the power "to regulate Commerce with foreign Nations, and among the several States." These seemingly dry words have enabled Congress to enact hundreds of laws that affect virtually every aspect of American life, including wages and hours, racial and other discrimination, public safety (air travel, for example), communications (radio, cable, television, and more), and thousands of other activities.

Presidential Interpretation. Presidents also have interpreted the Constitution in ways that have greatly expanded presidential power. Of all the parts of the document, the presidential powers have been seen by many students of the Constitution as the least well defined and therefore the most susceptible to aggressive expansion by holders of that office. For example, the president is named as "Commander in chief of the Army and Navy," which some presidents have used to commit American military forces to war without the approval of Congress. The Constitution also gives the president responsibility to take "Care that the Laws be faithfully executed," a grant so broad and so unconfined that it has allowed presidents to assume vast authority to direct the federal government's involvement in the lives of most Americans.

Judicial Interpretation. The role of the courts is crucial to defining the meaning of the Constitution's words and is closely interwoven with the actions of Congress and the president in interpreting the document. Judicial interpretation, particularly that of the Supreme Court, which is the final judicial word, also has been controversial in the nation's history because this power is held in the hands of a small number of people (nine in the case of the Supreme Court), none of whom is elected.

This extraordinary power, also called judicial review, is not explicitly stated in the Constitution, although there is evidence from the Constitutional Convention that a number of delegates assumed that the judiciary would have that authority. The power of the judiciary, and specifically the Supreme Court, to say what the

Constitution means was decided early in the Republic's history in one of the Court's most important cases—*Marbury v. Madison* (1803). In this case, the justices (then only six in number) read into the Constitution the power of the courts to declare acts of Congress in violation of the Constitution. Over the following two centuries, the principle has become accepted as a fundamental part of the process of government in the United States.

The examples of the Court's involvement in this area are many. One of the most important for modern times, as well as one of the most controversial, involves a constitutional amendment, the Fourteenth, adopted in the wake of the Civil War. This amendment, ratified July 9, 1868, states—among other things—that all persons born or naturalized in the United States are "citizens of the United States" and the state in which they live, and that no state can deprive anybody of "equal protection of the law." This is known today as the Equal Protection Clause.

The first part dealing with citizenship is an example of a constitutional amendment to reverse a decision by the Supreme Court, *Scott v. Sandford* (1857), which held that blacks were not citizens and were without constitutional rights. The Dred Scott case caused a huge public outcry and was an important event on the road to the Civil War.

The equal protection language also grew from the slavery issue of the day, but has become one of the most important and contentious parts of the Constitution as legislators and judges have struggled to give it meaning. It has been used to prohibit racial discrimination in public schools, require that districts from which persons are elected to Congress or state legislatures be equal in population, and—in one of the stickiest areas—state what is meant by affirmative action in hiring, college admissions, and other practices.

The Bill of Rights

The evolving Constitution is no better illustrated than by the Bill of Rights, the first ten amendments added to the document to calm the fears of many that the federal government would be too powerful. The Bill of Rights was written to prohibit actions by the federal government that would restrict individual rights, such as freedom of religion, speech, and the press. The Bill of Rights did not apply to the states, and did not for more than a century. The courts explicitly refused to nationalize the Bill of Rights. In the second century of the nation's history, however, the Supreme Court began to bring the states under some, but not all, of the provisions of the Bill of Rights. This process is known as selective incorporation, meaning that individual Court cases have been used to apply some of the rights in the first ten amendments to the actions of state governments.

The process began in 1833 with a case, *Barron v. Baltimore,* in which the Supreme Court was asked to apply to the states part of the Fifth Amendment that dealt with the government's seizure of private property. The Court refused, saying that "the fifth amendment to the constitution . . . is intended solely as a limitation on the exercise of power by the government of the United States, and is not applicable to the legislation of the states." The issue of applying the Bill of Rights to the states would not go away, however.

The adoption of the Fourteenth Amendment in 1868 changed the picture for those seeking ways to apply Bill of Rights protections to state government actions. That amendment, coming after the Civil War, was seen—correctly—as intended primarily through its citizenship and equal protection language to ensure the position and equality of blacks in the society. The amendment contained other language that applied to the conduct of state government authority: "No State shall make or enforce any law which shall abridge the privileges or immunities of citizens of the United States" and "Nor shall any State deprive any person of life, liberty, or property, without due process of law." What do these words mean? Slowly over the next century the Supreme Court has provided answers, although never a complete and final answer.

In the latter part of the nineteenth century, the Court in *The Slaughterhouse Cases* (1873) addressed whether a state's action (Louisiana) violated the Privileges and Immunities Clause. The answer was an emphatic "no." The Court said that the Privileges and Immunities Clause protected only national citizenship rights, and this interpretation has remained unchanged. The Due Process Clause has been another matter.

In another case, *Hurtado v. California* (1884), the Court rejected the claim of Joseph Hurtado that California, in charging him with murder, had violated provisions of the Fifth Amendment involving the same due process language used in the Fourteenth Amendment. The Court, citing *Barron,* did not accept Hurtado's argument that the state had violated his rights (his conviction was upheld) but allowed that the Due Process Clause would protect "fundamental principles of liberty and justice which lie at the base of all our civil and political institutions." That statement opened the door to debate about whether any or all of the Bill of Rights guarantees would meet this test.

In a 1908 decision *(Twining v. New Jersey)* a Court majority held that the Fourteenth Amendment's Due Process Clause might protect against state action certain rights similar to those in the Bill of Rights. The Court, cautiously, would not make the full Bill of Rights apply to the states but suggested that protections that could be identified as fundamental and inalienable might be made applicable to the states through the Fourteenth Amendment's Due Process Clause. It was a step down the road to incorporation of the Bill of Rights because it allowed future Courts to bring the principles of those ten amendments into play against state action toward their citizens.

From this point on lawyers would search intently for rights and freedoms that are fundamental and inalienable—or, as the Court stated in a later case, are such "that neither liberty nor justice would exist if they were sacrificed."

Using the case-by-case approach, the Supreme Court by the end of the 1960s had made most of the protections found in the Bill of Rights applicable to the states. At first, the extension was primarily of First Amendment freedoms of press, religion, and speech. In the 1960s the Court, under Chief Justice Earl Warren, turned its attention to the rights of persons accused of criminal activity. It made applicable to the states all of the major parts of the Bill of Rights intended to protect citizens against unfair and overreaching government actions, such as the following:

- The Fourth Amendment's guarantee against unreasonable search and seizure of a person or a person's home, car, or other personal space, and the rule that any evidence gathered by law enforcement officers in this manner could not be used in court to convict the person (the exclusionary rule).
- The Fifth Amendment's protection against self-incrimination or double jeopardy (being tried twice for the same crime).
- The Sixth Amendment's rights to a public trial, right to counsel (even if the defendant cannot afford a lawyer), trial by jury, confrontation of witnesses, and speedy trial.
- The Eighth Amendment's bar of cruel and unusual punishment.

The individual and personal liberties that underlie the Bill of Rights have provided the most dramatic examples in the latter part of the twentieth century of the evolution of the Constitution to address contemporary concerns. But it is not the only dramatic example. In the 1930s, the Supreme Court essentially did an about-face in its interpretation of the Constitution's words that apply to economic and business conduct in the nation. Until the 1930s the Court constructed elaborate doctrines that all but forbid the government from involvement in this area. But under the crisis of the Great Depression and the economic survival of the nation, the Court reversed itself and allowed the federal government to pass hundreds of laws, collectively known to history as the New Deal, that pushed the government deeply into the economic and business activities of America.

But however it came about—through formal amendment or interpretation by the courts, Congress, or the president—the U.S. Constitution has proven a remarkably consistent and stable and yet pliable document that Americans of all political persuasions have accepted as the basic law of the land.

Declaration of Independence

In Congress, July 4, 1776,
The Unanimous Declaration of the
Thirteen United States of America,

When in the Course of human events, it becomes necessary for one people to dissolve the political bands which have connected them with another, and to assume among the Powers of the earth, the separate and equal station to which the Laws of Nature and of Nature's God entitle them, a decent respect to the opinions of mankind requires that they should declare the causes which impel them to the separation.

We hold these truths to be self-evident, that all men are created equal, that they are endowed by their Creator with certain un-alienable Rights, that among these are Life, Liberty and the pursuit of Happiness. That to secure these rights, Governments are instituted among Men, deriving their just powers from the consent of the governed. That whenever any form of Government becomes destructive of these ends, it is the Right of the People to alter or to abolish it, and to institute new Government, laying its foundation on such principles and organizing its powers in such form, as to them shall seem most likely to effect their Safety and Happiness. Prudence, indeed, will dictate that Government long established should not be changed for light and transient causes; and accordingly all experience hath shown, that mankind are more disposed to suffer, while evils are sufferable, than to right themselves by abolishing the forms to which they are accustomed. But when a long train of abuses and usurpations, pursuing invariably the same Object evinces a design to reduce them under absolute Despotism, it is their right, it is their duty, to throw off such Government, and to provide new Guards for their future security. —Such has been the patient sufferance of these Colonies; and such is now the necessity which constrains them to alter their former Systems of Government. The history of the present King of Great Britain is a history of repeated injuries and usurpations, all having in direct object the establishment of an absolute Tyranny over these States. To prove this, let Facts be submitted to a candid world.

He has refused his Assent to Laws, the most wholesome and necessary for the public good.

He has forbidden his Governors to pass Laws of immediate and pressing importance, unless suspended in their operation till his Assent should be obtained; and when so suspended, he has utterly neglected to attend to them.

He has refused to pass other Laws for the accommodation of large districts of people, unless those people would relinquish the right of Representation in the Legislature, a right inestimable to them and formidable to tyrants only.

He has called together legislative bodies at places unusual, uncomfortable, and distant from the depository of their Public Records, for the sole purpose of fatiguing them into compliance with his measures.

He has dissolved Representative Houses repeatedly, for opposing with manly firmness his invasions on the rights of the people.

He has refused for a long time, after such dissolutions, to cause others to be elected; whereby the Legislative Powers, incapable of Annihilation, have returned to the People at large for their exercise; the State remaining in the mean time exposed to all the dangers of invasion from without, and convulsions within.

He has endeavored to prevent the population of these States; for that purpose obstructing the Laws of Naturalization of Foreigners; refusing to pass others to encourage their migration hither, and raising the conditions of new Appropriations of Lands.

He has obstructed the Administration of Justice, by refusing his Assent to Laws for establishing Judiciary Powers.

He has made Judges dependent on his Will alone, for the tenure of their offices, and the amount and payment of their salaries.

He has erected a multitude of New Offices, and sent hither swarms of Officers to harass our People, and eat out their substance.

He has kept among us, in times of peace, Standing Armies without the Consent of our legislature.

He has affected to render the Military independent of and superior to the Civil Power.

He has combined with others to subject us to a jurisdiction foreign to our constitution, and unacknowledged by our laws; giving his Assent to their acts of pretended legislation:

For quartering large bodies of armed troops among us:

For protecting them, by a mock Trial, from Punishment for any Murders which they should commit on the Inhabitants of these States:

For cutting off our Trade with all parts of the world:

For imposing taxes on us without our Consent:

For depriving us in many cases, of the benefits of Trial by Jury:

For transporting us beyond Seas to be tried for pretended offences:

For abolishing the free System of English Laws in a neighbouring Province, establishing therein an Arbitrary government, and enlarging its Boundaries so as to render it at once an example and fit instrument for introducing the same absolute rule into these Colonies:

For taking away our Charters, abolishing our most valuable Laws, and altering fundamentally the Forms of our Governments:

For suspending our own Legislature, and declaring themselves invested with Power to legislate for us in all cases whatsoever.

He has abdicated Government here, by declaring us out of his Protection and waging War against us.

He has plundered our seas, ravaged our Coasts, burnt our towns, and destroyed the lives of our people.

He is at this time transporting large armies of foreign mercenaries to compleat the works of death, desolation and tyranny, already begun with circumstances of Cruelty & perfidy scarcely paralleled in the most barbarous ages, and totally unworthy the Head of a civilized nation.

He has constrained our fellow Citizens taken Captive on the high Seas to bear Arms against their Country, to become the executioners of their friends and Brethren, or to fall themselves by their Hands.

He has excited domestic insurrections amongst us, and has endeavoured to bring on the inhabitants of our frontiers, the merciless Indian Savages, whose known rule of warfare, is an undistinguished destruction of all ages, sexes and conditions.

In every stage of these Oppressions We have Petitioned for Redress in the most humble terms: Our repeated Petitions have been answered only by repeated injury. A Prince, whose character is thus marked by every act which may define a Tyrant, is unfit to be the ruler of a free People.

Nor have We been wanting in attention to our British brethren. We have warned them from time to time of attempts by their legislature to extend an unwarrantable jurisdiction over us. We have reminded them of the circumstances of our emigration and settlement here. We have appealed to their native justice and magnanimity, and we have conjured them by the ties of our common kindred to disavow these usurpations, which would inevitably interrupt our connections and correspondence. They too have been deaf to the voice of justice and of consanguinity. We must, therefore, acquiesce in the necessity, which denounces our Separation, and hold them, as we hold the rest of mankind, Enemies in War, in Peace Friends.

We, therefore, the Representatives of the United States of America, in General Congress, Assembled, appealing to the Supreme Judge of the world for the rectitude of our intentions, do, in the Name, and by Authority of the good People of these Colonies, solemnly publish and declare, That these United Colonies are, and of Right ought to be Free and Independent States; that they are Absolved from all Allegiance to the British Crown, and that all political connection between them and the State of Great

Britain, is and ought to be totally dissolved; and that as Free and Independent States, they have full Power to levy War, conclude Peace, contract Alliances, establish Commerce, and to do all other Acts and Things which Independent States may of right do. And for the support of this Declaration, with a firm reliance on the Protection of Divine Providence, we mutually pledge to each other our Lives, our Fortunes and our sacred Honor.

JOHN HANCOCK.

New Hampshire:	Josiah Bartlett, William Whipple, Matthew Thornton.
Massachusetts-Bay:	Samuel Adams, John Adams, Robert Treat Paine, Elbridge Gerry.
Rhode Island:	Stephen Hopkins, William Ellery.
Connecticut:	Roger Sherman, Samuel Huntington, William Williams, Oliver Wolcott.
New York:	William Floyd, Philip Livingston, Francis Lewis, Lewis Morris.
Pennsylvania:	Robert Morris, Benjamin Harris, Benjamin Franklin, John Morton, George Clymer, James Smith,

George Taylor,
James Wilson,
George Ross.

Delaware:

Caesar Rodney,
George Read,
Thomas McKean.

Georgia:

Button Gwinnett,
Lyman Hall,
George Walton.

Maryland:

Samuel Chase,
William Paca,
Thomas Stone,
Charles Carroll of Carrollton.

Virginia:

George Wythe,
Richard Henry Lee,
Thomas Jefferson,
Benjamin Harrison,
Thomas Nelson Jr.,
Francis Lightfoot Lee,
Carter Braxton.

North Carolina:

William Hooper,
Joseph Hewes,
John Penn.

South Carolina:

Edward Rutledge,
Thomas Heyward Jr.,
Thomas Lynch Jr.,
Arthur Middleton.

New Jersey:

Richard Stockton,
John Witherspoon,
Francis Hopkinson,
John Hart,
Abraham Clark.

Organization of the Constitution of the United States

The original Constitution (Ratified by June 1788)

The Preamble

Article 1　The Legislative Department

Article 2　The Executive Department

Article 3　The Judicial Department

Article 4　Relations Between the States

Article 5　The Amendment Process

Article 6　General Provisions, Supremacy of Constitution

Article 7　Ratification of the Constitution

The Bill of Rights (Ratified 1791)

1　Freedom of religion, speech, press, assembly, petition

2　Militia and right to bear arms

3　Quartering of troops

4　Searches and seizures

5　Rights of accused persons

6　Criminal trials

7　Jury trials in common law cases

8　Reasonable bail and punishment

9　Rights reserved to the people

10　Powers reserved to the states

Later amendments

11　Suits against states (1795)

12　Elections of president and vice president (1804)

13　Slavery abolished (1865)

14　Protections, privileges of citizens of states (1868)

15   Voting rights of all races (1870)
16   Income tax power granted to Congress (1913)
17   Election of senators by the people (1913)
18   Prohibition of intoxicating beverages (1919)
19   Right to vote guaranteed to both sexes (1920)
20   "Lame duck" session of Congress eliminated (1933)
21   Repeal of eighteenth amendment (1933)
22   Limit on president's terms of office (1951)
23   Voting rights for District of Columbia (1961)
24   Prohibition on poll tax (1964)
25   Provision for disability of president (1967)
26   Voting age of eighteen (1971)
27   Compensation for senators and representatives (1992)

The Constitution of the United States

The Preamble

We the People of the United States, in Order to form a more perfect Union, establish Justice, insure domestic Tranquility, provide for the common defence, promote the general Welfare, and secure the Blessings of Liberty to ourselves and our Posterity, do ordain and establish this Constitution for the United States of America.

Article I

Section 1

All legislative Powers herein granted shall be vested in a Congress of the United States, which shall consist of a Senate and House of Representatives.

Section 2

1. The House of Representatives shall be composed of Members chosen every second Year by the People of the several States, and the Electors in each State shall have the Qualifications requisite for Electors of the most numerous Branch of the State Legislature.

2. No Person shall be a Representative who shall not have attained to the age of twenty five Years, and been seven Years a Citizen of the United States, and who shall not, when elected, be an Inhabitant of that State in which he shall be chosen.

3. [Representatives and direct Taxes shall be apportioned among the several States which may be included within this

Union, according to their respective Numbers, which shall be determined by adding to the whole Number of free Persons, including those bound to Service for a Term of Years, and excluding Indians not taxed, three fifths of all other Persons.]^1 The actual Enumeration shall be made within three Years after the first Meeting of the Congress of the United States, and within every subsequent Term of ten Years, in such Manner as they shall by Law direct. The Number of Representatives shall not exceed one for every thirty Thousand, but each State shall have at Least one Representative; and until such enumeration shall be made, the State of New Hampshire shall be entitled to chuse three, Massachusetts eight, Rhode-Island and Providence Plantations one, Connecticut five, New-York six, New Jersey four, Pennsylvania eight, Delaware one, Maryland six, Virginia tcn, North Carolina five, South Carolina five, and Georgia three.

4. When vacancies happen in the Representation from any State, the Executive Authority thereof shall issue Writs of Election to fill such Vacancies.

5. The House of Representatives shall chuse their Speaker and other Officers; and shall have the sole Power of Impeachment.

Section 3

1. The Senate of the United States shall be composed of two Senators from each State, [chosen by the Legislature thereof,]^2 for six Years; and each Senator shall have one Vote.

2. Immediately after they shall be assembled in Consequence of the first Election, they shall be divided as equally as may be into three Classes. The Seats of the Senators of the first Class shall be vacated at the Expiration of the second Year, of the second Class at the Expiration of the fourth Year, and of the third Class at the

---

1. The part in brackets was changed by section 2 of the Fourteenth Amendment.

2. The part in brackets was changed by the first paragraph of the Seventeenth Amendment.

Expiration of the sixth Year, so that one third may be chosen every second Year; [and if Vacancies happen by Resignation, or otherwise, during the Recess of the Legislature of any State, the Executive thereof may make temporary Appointments until the next Meeting of the Legislature, which shall then fill such Vacancies.]³

3. No Person shall be a Senator who shall not have attained to the Age of thirty Years, and been nine Years a Citizen of the United States, and who shall not, when elected, be an Inhabitant of that State for which he shall be chosen.

4. The Vice President of the United States shall be President of the Senate, but shall have no Vote, unless they be equally divided.

5. The Senate shall chuse their other Officers, and also a President pro tempore, in the Absence of the Vice President, or when he shall exercise the Office of President of the United States.

6. The Senate shall have the sole Power to try all Impeachments. When sitting for that Purpose, they shall be on Oath or Affirmation. When the President of the United States is tried, the Chief Justice shall preside: And no Person shall be convicted without the Concurrence of two thirds of the Members present.

7. Judgment in Cases of Impeachment shall not extend further than to removal from Office, and disqualification to hold and enjoy any Office of honor, Trust or Profit under the United States: but the Party convicted shall nevertheless be liable and subject to Indictment, Trial, Judgment and Punishment, according to Law.

Section 4

1. The Times, Places and Manner of holding Elections for Senators and Representatives, shall be prescribed in each State by the Legislature thereof; but the Congress may at any time by Law make or alter such Regulations, except as to the Places of chusing Senators.

---

3. The part in brackets was changed by the second paragraph of the Seventeenth Amendment.

2. The Congress shall assemble at least once in every Year, and such Meeting shall [be on the first Monday in December],[4] unless they shall by Law appoint a different Day.

Section 5

1. Each House shall be the Judge of the Elections, Returns and Qualifications of its own Members, and a Majority of each shall constitute a Quorum to do Business; but a smaller Number may adjourn from day to day, and may be authorized to compel the Attendance of absent Members, in such Manner, and under such Penalties as each House may provide.

2. Each House may determine the Rules of its Proceedings, punish its Members for disorderly Behaviour, and, with the Concurrence of two thirds, expel a Member.

3. Each House shall keep a Journal of its Proceedings, and from time to time publish the same, excepting such Parts as may in their Judgment require Secrecy; and the Yeas and Nays of the Members of either House on any question shall, at the Desire of one fifth of those Present, be entered on the Journal.

4. Neither House, during the Session of Congress, shall, without the Consent of the other, adjourn for more than three days, nor to any other Place than that in which the two Houses shall be sitting.

Section 6

1. The Senators and Representatives shall receive a Compensation for their Services, to be ascertained by Law, and paid out of the Treasury of the United States. They shall in all Cases, except Treason, Felony and Breach of the Peace, be privileged from Arrest during their Attendance at the Session of their respective Houses, and in going to and returning from the same; and for any

---

4. The part in brackets was changed by section 2 of the Twentieth Amendment.

Speech or Debate in either House, they shall not be questioned in any other Place.

2. No Senator or Representative shall, during the Time for which he was elected, be appointed to any civil Office under the Authority of the United States, which shall have been created, or the Emoluments whereof shall have been encreased during such time; and no Person holding any Office under the United States, shall be a Member of either House during his Continuance in Office.

Section 7

1. All Bills for raising Revenue shall originate in the House of Representatives; but the Senate may propose or concur with Amendments as on other Bills.

2. Every Bill which shall have passed the House of Representatives and the Senate, shall, before it become a Law, be presented to the President of the United States; If he approve he shall sign it, but if not he shall return it, with his Objections to that House in which it shall have originated, who shall enter the Objections at large on their Journal, and proceed to reconsider it. If after such Reconsideration two thirds of that House shall agree to pass the Bill, it shall be sent, together with the Objections, to the other House, by which it shall likewise be reconsidered, and if approved by two thirds of that House, it shall become a Law. But in all such Cases the Votes of both Houses shall be determined by yeas and Nays, and the Names of the Persons voting for and against the Bill shall be entered on the Journal of each House respectively. If any Bill shall not be returned by the President within ten Days (Sundays excepted) after it shall have been presented to him, the Same shall be a Law, in like Manner as if he had signed it, unless the Congress by their Adjournment prevent its Return, in which Case it shall not be a Law.

3. Every Order, Resolution, or Vote to which the Concurrence of the Senate and House of Representatives may be necessary (except on a question of Adjournment) shall be presented to the

President of the United States; and before the Same shall take Effect, shall be approved by him, or being disapproved by him, shall be repassed by two thirds of the Senate and House of Representatives, according to the Rules and Limitations prescribed in the Case of a Bill.

Section 8

1. The Congress shall have Power To lay and collect Taxes, Duties, Imposts and Excises, to pay the Debts and provide for the common Defence and general Welfare of the United States; but all Duties, Imposts and Excises shall be uniform throughout the United States;

2. To borrow Money on the credit of the United States;

3. To regulate Commerce with foreign Nations, and among the several States, and with the Indian Tribes;

4. To establish an uniform Rule of Naturalization, and uniform Laws on the subject of Bankruptcies throughout the United States;

5. To coin Money, regulate the Value thereof, and of foreign Coin, and fix the Standard of Weights and Measures;

6. To provide for the Punishment of counterfeiting the Securities and current Coin of the United States;

7. To establish Post Offices and post Roads;

8. To promote the Progress of Science and useful Arts, by securing for limited Times to Authors and Inventors the exclusive Right to their respective Writings and Discoveries;

9. To constitute Tribunals inferior to the supreme Court;

10. To define and punish Piracies and Felonies committed on the high Seas, and Offences against the Law of Nations;

11. To declare War, grant Letters of Marque and Reprisal, and make Rules concerning Captures on Land and Water;

12. To raise and support Armies, but no Appropriation of Money to that Use shall be for a longer Term than two Years;

13. To provide and maintain a Navy;

14. To make Rules for the Government and Regulation of the land and naval Forces;

15. To provide for calling forth the Militia to execute the Laws of the Union, suppress Insurrections and repel Invasions;

16. To provide for organizing, arming, and disciplining, the Militia, and for governing such Part of them as may be employed in the Service of the United States, reserving to the States respectively, the Appointment of the Officers, and the Authority of training the Militia according to the discipline prescribed by Congress;

17. To exercise exclusive Legislation in all Cases whatsoever, over such District (not exceeding ten Miles square) as may, by Cession of particular States, and the Acceptance of Congress, become the Seat of the Government of the United States, and to exercise like Authority over all Places purchased by the Consent of the Legislature of the State in which the Same shall be, for the Erection of Forts, Magazines, Arsenals, dock-Yards, and other needful Buildings; —And

18. To make all Laws which shall be necessary and proper for carrying into Execution the foregoing Powers, and all other Powers vested by this Constitution in the Government of the United States, or in any Department or Officer thereof.

Section 9

1. The Migration or Importation of such Persons as any of the States now existing shall think proper to admit, shall not be prohibited by the Congress prior to the Year one thousand eight hundred and eight, but a Tax or duty may be imposed on such Importation, not exceeding ten dollars for each Person.

2. The Privilege of the Writ of Habeas Corpus shall not be suspended, unless when in Cases of Rebellion or Invasion the public Safety may require it.

3. No Bill of Attainder or ex post facto Law shall be passed.

4. No Capitation, or other direct, Tax shall be laid, unless in Proportion to the Census or Enumeration herein before directed to be taken.[5]

5. No Tax or Duty shall be laid on Articles exported from any State.

6. No Preference shall be given by any Regulation of Commerce or Revenue to the Ports of one State over those of another; nor shall Vessels bound to, or from, one State, be obliged to enter, clear, or pay Duties in another.

7. No Money shall be drawn from the Treasury, but in Consequence of Appropriations made by Law; and a regular Statement and Account of the Receipts and Expenditures of all public Money shall be published from time to time.

8. No Title of Nobility shall be granted by the United States: And no Person holding any Office of Profit or Trust under them, shall, without the Consent of the Congress, accept of any present, Emolument, Office, or Title, of any kind whatever, from any King, Prince, or foreign State.

Section 10

1. No State shall enter into any Treaty, Alliance, or Confederation; grant Letters of Marque and Reprisal; coin Money; emit Bills of Credit; make any Thing but gold and silver Coin a Tender in Payment of Debts; pass any Bill of Attainder, ex post facto Law, or Law impairing the Obligation of Contracts, or grant any Title of Nobility.

2. No State shall, without the Consent of the Congress, lay any Imposts or Duties on Imports or Exports, except what may be absolutely necessary for executing it's inspection Laws: and the net Produce of all Duties and Imposts, laid by any State on Imports or Exports, shall be for the Use of the Treasury of the United

---

5. The Sixteenth Amendment gave Congress the power to tax incomes.

States; and all such Laws shall be subject to the Revision and Controul of the Congress.

3. No State shall, without the Consent of Congress, lay any Duty of Tonnage, keep Troops, or Ships of War in time of Peace, enter into any Agreement or Compact with another State, or with a foreign Power, or engage in War, unless actually invaded, or in such imminent Danger as will not admit of delay.

Article II

Section 1

1. The executive Power shall be vested in a President of the United States of America. He shall hold his Office during the Term of four Years, and, together with the Vice President, chosen for the same Term, be elected, as follows:

2. Each State shall appoint, in such Manner as the Legislature thereof may direct, a Number of Electors, equal to the whole Number of Senators and Representatives to which the State may be entitled in the Congress: but no Senator or Representative, or Person holding an Office of Trust or Profit under the United States, shall be appointed an Elector.

3. [The Electors shall meet in their respective States, and vote by Ballot for two Persons, of whom one at least shall not be an Inhabitant of the same State with themselves. And they shall make a List of all the Persons voted for, and of the Number of Votes for each; which List they shall sign and certify, and transmit sealed to the Seat of the Government of the United States, directed to the President of the Senate. The President of the Senate shall, in the Presence of the Senate and House of Representatives, open all the Certificates, and the Votes shall then be counted. The Person having the greatest Number of Votes shall be the President, if such Number be a Majority of the whole Number of Electors appointed; and if there be more than one who have such Majority, and have an equal Number of Votes, then the House of Represen-

tatives shall immediately chuse by Ballot one of them for President; and if no Person have a Majority, then from the five highest on the list the said House shall in like Manner chuse the President. But in chusing the President, the Votes shall be taken by States, the Representation from each State having one Vote; A quorum for this Purpose shall consist of a Member or Members from two thirds of the States, and a Majority of all the States shall be necessary to a Choice. In every Case, after the Choice of the President, the Person having the greatest Number of Votes of the Electors shall be the Vice President. But if there should remain two or more who have equal Votes, the Senate shall chuse from them by Ballot the Vice President.][6]

4. The Congress may determine the Time of chusing the Electors, and the Day on which they shall give their Votes; which Day shall be the same throughout the United States.

5. No Person except a natural born Citizen, or a Citizen of the United States, at the time of the Adoption of this Constitution, shall be eligible to the Office of President; neither shall any Person be eligible to that Office who shall not have attained to the Age of thirty five Years, and been fourteen Years a Resident within the United States.

6. In Case of the Removal of the President from Office, or of his Death, Resignation, or Inability to discharge the Powers and Duties of the said Office,[7] the Same shall devolve on the Vice President, and the Congress may by Law provide for the Case of Removal, Death, Resignation or Inability, both of the President and Vice President, declaring what Officer shall then act as President, and such Officer shall act accordingly, until the Disability be removed, or a President shall be elected.

7. The President shall, at stated Times, receive for his Services, a Compensation, which shall neither be encreased nor diminished during the Period for which he shall have been elected, and he

---

6. The material in brackets has been superseded by the Twelfth Amendment.

7. This provision has been affected by the Twenty-fifth Amendment.

shall not receive within that Period any other Emolument from the United States, or any of them.

8. Before he enter on the Execution of his Office, he shall take the following Oath or Affirmation:—"I do solemnly swear (or affirm) that I will faithfully execute the Office of President of the United States, and will to the best of my Ability, preserve, protect and defend the Constitution of the United States."

Section 2

1. The President shall be Commander in Chief of the Army and Navy of the United States, and of the Militia of the several States, when called into the actual Service of the United States; he may require the Opinion, in writing, of the principal Officer in each of the executive Departments, upon any Subject relating to the Duties of their respective Offices, and he shall have Power to grant Reprieves and Pardons for Offences against the United States, except in Cases of Impeachment.

2. He shall have Power, by and with the Advice and Consent of the Senate, to make Treaties, provided two thirds of the Senators present concur; and he shall nominate, and by and with the Advice and Consent of the Senate, shall appoint Ambassadors, other public Ministers and Consuls, Judges of the supreme Court, and all other Officers of the United States, whose Appointments are not herein otherwise provided for, and which shall be established by Law: but the Congress may by Law vest the Appointment of such inferior Officers, as they think proper, in the President alone, in the Courts of Law, or in the Heads of Departments.

3. The President shall have Power to fill up all Vacancies that may happen during the Recess of the Senate, by granting Commissions which shall expire at the End of their next Session.

Section 3

He shall from time to time give to the Congress Information of the State of the Union, and recommend to their Consideration such Measures as he shall judge necessary and expedient; he may, on extraordinary Occasions, convene both Houses, or either of them, and in Case of Disagreement between them, with Respect to the Time of Adjournment, he may adjourn them to such Time as he shall think proper; he shall receive Ambassadors and other public Ministers; he shall take Care that the Laws be faithfully executed, and shall Commission all the Officers of the United States.

Section 4

The President, Vice President and all civil Officers of the United States, shall be removed from Office on Impeachment for, and Conviction of, Treason, Bribery, or other high Crimes and Misdemeanors.

Article III

Section 1

The judicial Power of the United States, shall be vested in one supreme Court, and in such inferior Courts as the Congress may from time to time ordain and establish. The Judges, both of the supreme and inferior Courts, shall hold their Offices during good Behaviour, and shall, at stated Times, receive for their Services, a Compensation, which shall not be diminished during their Continuance in Office.

Section 2

1. The judicial Power shall extend to all Cases, in Law and Equity, arising under this Constitution, the Laws of the United States, and Treaties made, or which shall be made, under their Authority;—to all Cases affecting Ambassadors, other public Ministers and Consuls;—to all Cases of admiralty and maritime Jurisdiction;—to Controversies to which the United States shall

be a Party;—to Controversies between two or more States;—between a State and Citizens of another State;[8]—between Citizens of different States;—between Citizens of the same State claiming Lands under Grants of different States, and between a State, or the Citizens thereof, and foreign States, Citizens or Subjects.[8]

2. In all Cases affecting Ambassadors, other public Ministers and Consuls, and those in which a State shall be Party, the supreme Court shall have original Jurisdiction. In all the other Cases before mentioned, the supreme Court shall have appellate Jurisdiction, both as to Law and Fact, with such Exceptions, and under such Regulations as the Congress shall make.

3. The Trial of all Crimes, except in Cases of Impeachment, shall be by Jury; and such Trial shall be held in the State where the said Crimes shall have been committed; but when not committed within any State, the Trial shall be at such Place or Places as the Congress may by Law have directed.

Section 3

1. Treason against the United States, shall consist only in levying War against them, or in adhering to their Enemies, giving them Aid and Comfort. No Person shall be convicted of Treason unless on the Testimony of two Witnesses to the same overt Act, or on Confession in open Court.

2. The Congress shall have Power to declare the Punishment of Treason, but no Attainder of Treason shall work Corruption of Blood, or Forfeiture except during the Life of the Person attainted.

Article IV

Section 1

Full Faith and Credit shall be given in each State to the public Acts, Records, and judicial Proceedings of every other State. And

---

8. These clauses were affected by the Eleventh Amendment.

the Congress may by general Laws prescribe the Manner in which such Acts, Records and Proceedings shall be proved, and the Effect thereof.

Section 2

1. The Citizens of each State shall be entitled to all Privileges and Immunities of Citizens in the several States.

2. A Person charged in any State with Treason, Felony, or other Crime, who shall flee from Justice, and be found in another State, shall on Demand of the executive Authority of the State from which he fled, be delivered up, to be removed to the State having Jurisdiction of the Crime.

3. [No Person held to Service or Labour in one State, under the Laws thereof, escaping into another, shall, in Consequence of any Law or Regulation therein, be discharged from such Service or Labour, but shall be delivered up on Claim of the Party to whom such Service or Labour may be due.][9]

Section 3

1. New States may be admitted by the Congress into this Union; but no new State shall be formed or erected within the Jurisdiction of any other State; nor any State be formed by the Junction of two or more States, or Parts of States, without the Consent of the Legislatures of the States concerned as well as of the Congress.

2. The Congress shall have Power to dispose of and make all needful Rules and Regulations respecting the Territory or other Property belonging to the United States; and nothing in this Constitution shall be so construed as to Prejudice any Claims of the United States, or of any particular State.

---

9. This paragraph has been superseded by the Thirteenth Amendment.

Section 4

The United States shall guarantee to every State in this Union a Republican Form of Government, and shall protect each of them against Invasion; and on Application of the Legislature, or of the Executive (when the Legislature cannot be convened) against domestic Violence.

Article V

The Congress, whenever two thirds of both Houses shall deem it necessary, shall propose Amendments to this Constitution, or, on the Application of the Legislatures of two thirds of the several States, shall call a Convention for proposing Amendments, which, in either Case, shall be valid to all Intents and Purposes, as Part of this Constitution, when ratified by the Legislatures of three fourths of the several States, or by Conventions in three fourths thereof, as the one or the other Mode of Ratification may be proposed by the Congress; Provided [that no Amendment which may be made prior to the Year One thousand eight hundred and eight shall in any Manner affect the first and fourth Clauses in the Ninth Section of the first Article; and][10] that no State, without its Consent, shall be deprived of its equal Suffrage in the Senate.

Article VI

1. All Debts contracted and Engagements entered into, before the Adoption of this Constitution, shall be as valid against the United States under this Constitution, as under the Confederation.

2. This Constitution, and the Laws of the United States which shall be made in Pursuance thereof; and all Treaties made, or which shall be made, under the Authority of the United States, shall be the supreme Law of the Land; and the Judges in every

---

10. Obsolete.

State shall be bound thereby, any Thing in the Constitution or Laws of any State to the Contrary notwithstanding.

3. The Senators and Representatives before mentioned, and the Members of the several State Legislatures, and all executive and judicial Officers, both of the United States and of the several States, shall be bound by Oath or Affirmation, to support this Constitution; but no religious Test shall ever be required as a Qualification to any Office or public Trust under the United States.

Article VII

The Ratification of the Conventions of nine States, shall be sufficient for the Establishment of this Constitution between the States so ratifying the Same.

Done in Convention by the Unanimous Consent of the States present the Seventeenth Day of September in the Year of our Lord one thousand seven hundred and Eighty seven and of the Independence of the United States of America the Twelfth. IN WITNESS whereof We have hereunto subscribed our Names,

George Washington,
President and
deputy from Virginia.

New Hampshire:	John Langdon, Nicholas Gilman.
Massachusetts:	Nathaniel Gorham, Rufus King.
Connecticut:	William Samuel Johnson, Roger Sherman.
New York:	Alexander Hamilton.

New Jersey:	William Livingston, David Brearley, William Paterson, Jonathan Dayton.
Pennsylvania:	Benjamin Franklin, Thomas Mifflin, Robert Morris, George Clymer, Thomas FitzSimons, Jared Ingersoll, James Wilson, Gouverneur Morris.
Delaware:	George Read, Gunning Bedford Jr., John Dickinson, Richard Bassett, Jacob Broom.
Maryland:	James McHenry, Daniel of St. Thomas Jenifer, Daniel Carroll.
Virginia:	John Blair, James Madison Jr.
North Carolina:	William Blount, Richard Dobbs Spaight, Hugh Williamson.
South Carolina:	John Rutledge, Charles Cotesworth Pinckney, Charles Pinckney, Pierce Butler.
Georgia:	William Few, Abraham Baldwin.

[The language of the original Constitution, not including the Amendments, was adopted by a convention of the states on September 17, 1787, and was subsequently ratified by the states on the following dates: Delaware, December 7, 1787; Pennsylvania, December 12, 1787; New Jersey, December 18, 1787; Georgia, January 2, 1788; Connecticut, January 9, 1788; Massachusetts, February 6, 1788; Maryland, April 28, 1788; South Carolina, May 23, 1788; New Hampshire, June 21, 1788.

Ratification was completed on June 21, 1788.

The Constitution subsequently was ratified by Virginia, June 25, 1788; New York, July 26, 1788; North Carolina, November 21, 1789; Rhode Island, May 29, 1790; and Vermont, January 10, 1791.]

Amendments

Amendment I

(First ten amendments ratified December 15, 1791.)

Congress shall make no law respecting an establishment of religion, or prohibiting the free exercise thereof; or abridging the freedom of speech, or of the press; or the right of the people peaceably to assemble, and to petition the Government for a redress of grievances.

Amendment II

A well regulated Militia, being necessary to the security of a free State, the right of the people to keep and bear Arms, shall not be infringed.

Amendment III

No Soldier shall, in time of peace be quartered in any house, without the consent of the Owner, nor in time of war, but in a manner to be prescribed by law.

Amendment IV

The right of the people to be secure in their persons, houses, papers, and effects, against unreasonable searches and seizures, shall not be violated, and no Warrants shall issue, but upon probable cause, supported by Oath or affirmation, and particularly describing the place to be searched, and the persons or things to be seized.

Amendment V

No person shall be held to answer for a capital, or otherwise infamous crime, unless on a presentment or indictment of a Grand Jury, except in cases arising in the land or naval forces, or in the Militia, when in actual service in time of War or public danger; nor shall any person be subject for the same offence to be twice put in jeopardy of life or limb; nor shall be compelled in any criminal case to be a witness against himself, nor be deprived of life, liberty, or property, without due process of law; nor shall private property be taken for public use, without just compensation.

Amendment VI

In all criminal prosecutions, the accused shall enjoy the right to a speedy and public trial, by an impartial jury of the State and district wherein the crime shall have been committed, which district shall have been previously ascertained by law, and to be informed of the nature and cause of the accusation; to be confronted with the witnesses against him; to have compulsory process for obtaining witnesses in his favor, and to have the Assistance of Counsel for his defence.

Amendment VII

In Suits at common law, where the value in controversy shall exceed twenty dollars, the right of trial by jury shall be preserved, and no fact tried by a jury, shall be otherwise re-examined in any Court of the United States, than according to the rules of the common law.

Amendment VIII

Excessive bail shall not be required, nor excessive fines imposed, nor cruel and unusual punishments inflicted.

Amendment IX

The enumeration in the Constitution, of certain rights, shall not be construed to deny or disparage others retained by the people.

Amendment X

The powers not delegated to the United States by the Constitution, nor prohibited by it to the States, are reserved to the States respectively, or to the people.

Amendment XI *(Ratified February 7, 1795)*

The Judicial power of the United States shall not be construed to extend to any suit in law or equity, commenced or prosecuted against one of the United States by Citizens of another State, or by Citizens or Subjects of any Foreign State.

Amendment XII *(Ratified June 15, 1804)*

The Electors shall meet in their respective states and vote by ballot for President and Vice-President, one of whom, at least, shall not be an inhabitant of the same state with themselves; they shall name in their ballots the person voted for as President, and in distinct ballots the person voted for as Vice-President, and they shall make distinct lists of all persons voted for as President, and of all persons voted for as Vice-President, and of the number of votes for each, which lists they shall sign and certify, and transmit sealed to the seat of the government of the United States, directed to the President of the Senate;— The President of the Senate shall, in the presence of the Senate and House of Representatives, open all the certificates and the votes shall then be counted;—The person having the greatest number of votes for President, shall be the President, if such number be a majority of the whole number of Electors appointed; and if no person have such majority, then from the persons having the highest numbers not exceeding three on the list of those voted for as President, the House of Representatives shall choose immediately, by ballot, the President. But in choosing the President, the votes shall be taken by states, the representation from each state having one vote; a quorum for this purpose shall consist of a member or members from two-thirds of the states, and a majority of all the states shall be necessary to a choice. [And if the House of Representatives shall not choose a President whenever the right of choice shall devolve upon them, before the fourth day of March next following, then the Vice-President shall act as President, as in the case of the death or other constitutional disability of the President.—][11] The person having the greatest number of votes as Vice-President, shall be the Vice-President, if such number be a majority of the whole number of Electors appointed, and if no person have a majority, then from the two highest numbers on the list, the Senate shall choose the Vice-President; a quorum for the purpose shall consist of two-thirds of the whole number of Senators, and a majority of the whole number shall be necessary to a choice. But no person constitutionally ineligible to the office of President shall be eligible to that of Vice-President of the United States.

---

11. The part in brackets has been superseded by section 3 of the Twentieth Amendment.

Amendment XIII *(Ratified December 6, 1865)*

Section 1. Neither slavery nor involuntary servitude, except as a punishment for crime whereof the party shall have been duly convicted, shall exist within the United States, or any place subject to their jurisdiction.

Section 2. Congress shall have power to enforce this article by appropriate legislation.

Amendment XIV *(Ratified July 9, 1868)*

Section 1. All persons born or naturalized in the United States, and subject to the jurisdiction thereof, are citizens of the United States and of the State wherein they reside. No State shall make or enforce any law which shall abridge the privileges or immunities of citizens of the United States; nor shall any State deprive any person of life, liberty, or property, without due process of law; nor deny to any person within its jurisdiction the equal protection of the laws.

Section 2. Representatives shall be apportioned among the several States according to their respective numbers, counting the whole number of persons in each State, excluding Indians not taxed. But when the right to vote at any election for the choice of electors for President and Vice President of the United States, Representatives in Congress, the Executive and Judicial officers of a State, or the members of the Legislature thereof, is denied to any of the male inhabitants of such State, being twenty-one years of age,[12] and citizens of the United States, or in any way abridged, except for participation in rebellion, or other crime, the basis of representation therein shall be reduced in the proportion which

---

12. See the Nineteenth and Twenty-sixth Amendments.

the number of such male citizens shall bear to the whole number of male citizens twenty-one years of age in such State.

Section 3. No person shall be a Senator or Representative in Congress, or elector of President and Vice President, or hold any office, civil or military, under the United States, or under any State, who, having previously taken an oath, as a member of Congress, or as an officer of the United States, or as a member of any State legislature, or as an executive or judicial officer of any State, to support the Constitution of the United States, shall have engaged in insurrection or rebellion against the same, or given aid or comfort to the enemies thereof. But Congress may by a vote of two-thirds of each House, remove such disability.

Section 4. The validity of the public debt of the United States, authorized by law, including debts incurred for payment of pensions and bounties for services in suppressing insurrection or rebellion, shall not be questioned. But neither the United States nor any State shall assume or pay any debt or obligation incurred in aid of insurrection or rebellion against the United States, or any claim for the loss or emancipation of any slave; but all such debts, obligations and claims shall be held illegal and void.

Section 5. The Congress shall have power to enforce, by appropriate legislation, the provisions of this article.

Amendment XV *(Ratified February 3, 1870)*

Section 1. The right of citizens of the United States to vote shall not be denied or abridged by the United States or by any State on account of race, color, or previous condition of servitude.

Section 2. The Congress shall have power to enforce this article by appropriate legislation.

Amendment XVI *(Ratified February 3, 1913)*

The Congress shall have power to lay and collect taxes on incomes, from whatever source derived, without apportionment among the several States, and without regard to any census or enumeration.

Amendment XVII *(Ratified April 8, 1913)*

The Senate of the United States shall be composed of two Senators from each State, elected by the people thereof, for six years; and each Senator shall have one vote. The electors in each State shall have the qualifications requisite for electors of the most numerous branch of the State legislatures.

When vacancies happen in the representation of any State in the Senate, the executive authority of such State shall issue writs of election to fill such vacancies: *Provided,* That the legislature of any State may empower the executive thereof to make temporary appointments until the people fill the vacancies by election as the legislature may direct.

This amendment shall not be so construed as to affect the election or term of any Senator chosen before it becomes valid as part of the Constitution.

Amendment XVIII *(Ratified January 16, 1919)*

Section 1. After one year from the ratification of this article the manufacture, sale, or transportation of intoxicating liquors within, the importation thereof into, or the exportation thereof from the United States and all territory subject to the jurisdiction thereof for beverage purposes is hereby prohibited.

Section 2. The Congress and the several States shall have concurrent power to enforce this article by appropriate legislation.

Section 3. This article shall be inoperative unless it shall have been ratified as an amendment to the Constitution by the legislatures of the several States, as provided in the Constitution, within seven years from the date of the submission hereof to the States by the Congress.][13]

Amendment XIX *(Ratified August 18, 1920)*

The right of citizens of the United States to vote shall not be denied or abridged by the United States or by any State on account of sex.

Congress shall have power to enforce this article by appropriate legislation.

Amendment XX *(Ratified January 23, 1933)*

Section 1. The terms of the President and Vice President shall end at noon on the 20th day of January, and the terms of Senators and Representatives at noon on the 3d day of January, of the years in which such terms would have ended if this article had not been ratified; and the terms of their successors shall then begin.

Section 2. The Congress shall assemble at least once in every year, and such meeting shall begin at noon on the 3d day of January, unless they shall by law appoint a different day.

Section 3.[14] If, at the time fixed for the beginning of the term of the President, the President elect shall have died, the Vice President elect shall become President. If a President shall not have been chosen before the time fixed for the beginning of his term, or

---

13. This Amendment was repealed by section 1 of the Twenty-first Amendment.

14. See the Twenty-fifth Amendment.

if the President elect shall have failed to qualify, then the Vice President elect shall act as President until a President shall have qualified; and the Congress may by law provide for the case wherein neither a President elect nor a Vice President elect shall have qualified, declaring who shall then act as President, or the manner in which one who is to act shall be selected, and such person shall act accordingly until a President or Vice President shall have qualified.

Section 4. The Congress may by law provide for the case of the death of any of the persons from whom the House of Representatives may choose a President whenever the right of choice shall have devolved upon them, and for the case of the death of any of the persons from whom the Senate may choose a Vice President whenever the right of choice shall have devolved upon them.

Section 5. Sections 1 and 2 shall take effect on the 15th day of October following the ratification of this article.

Section 6. This article shall be inoperative unless it shall have been ratified as an amendment to the Constitution by the legislatures of three-fourths of the several States within seven years from the date of its submission.

Amendment XXI *(Ratified December 5, 1933)*

Section 1. The eighteenth article of amendment to the Constitution of the United States is hereby repealed.

Section 2. The transportation or importation into any State, Territory, or possession of the United States for delivery or use therein of intoxicating liquors, in violation of the laws thereof, is hereby prohibited.

Section 3. This article shall be inoperative unless it shall have been ratified as an amendment to the Constitution by conventions in the several States, as provided in the Constitution, within seven years from the date of the submission hereof to the States by the Congress.

Amendment XXII *(Ratified February 27, 1951)*

Section 1. No person shall be elected to the office of the President more than twice, and no person who has held the office of President, or acted as President, for more than two years of a term to which some other person was elected President shall be elected to the office of the President more than once. But this Article shall not apply to any person holding the office of President when this Article was proposed by the Congress, and shall not prevent any person who may be holding the office of President, or acting as President, during the term within which this Article become operative from holding the office of President or acting as President during the remainder of such term.

Section 2. This article shall be inoperative unless it shall have been ratified as an amendment to the Constitution by the legislatures of three-fourths of the several States within seven years from the date of its submission to the States by the Congress.

Amendment XXIII *(Ratified March 29, 1961)*

Section 1. The District constituting the seat of Government of the United States shall appoint in such manner as the Congress may direct:

A number of electors of President and Vice President equal to the whole number of Senators and Representatives in Congress to which the District would be entitled if it were a State, but in no event more than the least populous State; they shall be in addition to those appointed by the States, but they shall be considered, for the purposes of the election of President and Vice President, to be electors appointed by a State; and they shall meet in the District and perform such duties as provided by the twelfth article of amendment.

Section 2. The Congress shall have power to enforce this article by appropriate legislation.

Amendment XXIV *(Ratified January 23, 1964)*

Section 1. The right of citizens of the United States to vote in any primary or other election for President or Vice President, for electors for President or Vice President, or for Senator or Representative in Congress, shall not be denied or abridged by the United States or any State by reason of failure to pay any poll tax or other tax.

Section 2. The Congress shall have power to enforce this article by appropriate legislation.

Amendment XXV *(Ratified February 10, 1967)*

Section 1. In case of the removal of the President from office or of his death or resignation, the Vice President shall become President.

Section 2. Whenever there is a vacancy in the office of the Vice President, the President shall nominate a Vice President who shall take office upon confirmation by a majority vote of both Houses of Congress.

Section 3. Whenever the President transmits to the President pro tempore of the Senate and the Speaker of the House of

Representatives his written declaration that he is unable to discharge the powers and duties of his office, and until he transmits to them a written declaration to the contrary, such powers and duties shall be discharged by the Vice President as Acting President.

Section 4. Whenever the Vice President and a majority of either the principal officers of the executive departments or of such other body as Congress may by law provide, transmit to the President pro tempore of the Senate and the Speaker of the House of Representatives their written declaration that the President is unable to discharge the powers and duties of his office, the Vice President shall immediately assume the powers and duties of the office as Acting President.

Thereafter, when the President transmits to the President pro tempore of the Senate and the Speaker of the House of Representatives his written declaration that no inability exists, he shall resume the powers and duties of his office unless the Vice President and a majority of either the principal officers of the executive department or of such other body as Congress may by law provide, transmit within four days to the President pro tempore of the Senate and the Speaker of the House of Representatives their written declaration that the President is unable to discharge the powers and duties of his office. Thereupon Congress shall decide the issue, assembling within forty-eight hours for that purpose if not in session. If the Congress, within twenty-one days after receipt of the latter written declaration, or, if Congress is not in session, within twenty-one days after Congress is required to assemble, determines by two-thirds vote of both Houses that the President is unable to discharge the powers and duties of his office, the Vice President shall continue to discharge the same as Acting President; otherwise, the President shall resume the powers and duties of his office.

Amendment XXVI *(Ratified July 1, 1971)*

Section 1. The right of citizens of the United States, who are eighteen years of age or older, to vote shall not be denied or abridged by the United States or by any State on account of age.

Section 2. The Congress shall have power to enforce this article by appropriate legislation.

Amendment XXVII *(Ratified May 7, 1992)*

No law varying the compensation for the services of the Senators and Representatives shall take effect, until an election of Representatives shall have intervened.

Source: U.S. Congress, House, Committee on the Judiciary, *The Constitution of the United States of America, as Amended,* 100th Cong., 1st sess., 1987, H Doc 100-94.

Index to the Constitution of the United States

	Art.	Sect.	Para.

A

E

J

L

R

S

Notes

Note A

The Supreme Court's Power of Judicial Review

Courts often are called upon to review cases in which there is a dispute as to whether a law or a government official's action is permitted under the Constitution. The Supreme Court has the final word in such cases. For this reason, the Court is a major factor in the balance of power among the three branches of government established by the Constitution. Under the power of judicial review, for example, the Court may rule on the legality of a town's zoning law, a lower court's conduct of a trial, a school board regulation, or an action by a policeman or the president of the United States.

This power is not provided for directly in the Constitution. The Court itself defined it in 1803 in the case *Marbury v. Madison.* Chief Justice John Marshall wrote the opinion. It declared that judicial review is the outgrowth of English and American legal traditions along with certain provisions of the Constitution itself. The reasoning was that courts first must decide what laws mean in order to rule on cases arising under them; that the Supreme Court must decide the meaning of the Constitution in order to defend it as the "supreme law of the land"; and, finally, it must decide whether a law or action is in agreement with the Constitution, because it may recognize only laws which are made in pursuance of that basic law, according to Article VI, Paragraph 2. If the Court finds that a law or action is not in agreement with the Constitution, it can declare it unconstitutional and unenforceable.

Note B

The Power of Congress to Investigate

In order to carry out its functions, Congress must gather information. Such functions include passing laws on a vast variety of subjects, approving treaties, evaluating individuals nominated by the president, and appropriating money for carrying out the programs of government. Closely associated with this is the authority to require individuals to appear and provide necessary information—the subpoena power.

Although the investigating power is not specifically provided for in the Constitution, it has been considered part of our law-making tradition from the earlier state legislatures and the English Parliament. It is a significant power in the check and balance system. There are limits to it, however. The Supreme Court has said that the Congress may not investigate to restrict the First Amendment rights of individuals or to attempt to exercise powers assigned to the executive and judicial departments.

Note C

The Power of Congress to Change the Size of the Supreme Court

The Constitution says nothing about the size of the Supreme Court or whether it can be changed from time to time. Under Article III, Section 1, Congress established the judicial system in the Judiciary Act of 1789. It established a six-member court. At various times since, the size has been changed to seven, ten, and the present nine members. The Court has made no ruling on the subject.

Background for the notes has been obtained from Edward S. Corwin, and Jack W. Peltason, *Understanding the Constitution* (New York: Holt, Rinehart, & Winston, 1964).

A Glossary of Terms in the Constitution of the United States

Abridge	To reduce, deprive, or cut off.
Adjourn	To halt a meeting temporarily.
Admiralty	Admiralty laws apply to shipping and disputes and offenses committed on the high seas; also to matters on public waters within the country, such as the Great Lakes.
Affirmation	A solemn declaration that serves for those whose beliefs will not permit the swearing of an oath.
Alliance	An agreement between two or more nations to come to the defense of any partner that is attacked.
Apportion	To divide up or distribute in proportion to something. In this case, the larger the population of a state, the more representatives it has and the more taxes come from it.
Appropriations	Money set aside by government for specific uses, such as military forces or highway construction.
Ascertain	To obtain information.
Attainder	Guilt. A bill of attainder is a law declaring someone guilty of an offense without a trial.
Bankruptcy	Unable to pay one's debts. Bankruptcy laws provide a fair and orderly way to divide up the bankrupt person's remaining property among those to whom money is owed.

Bill	Term that describes a proposal being discussed and debated in Congress. When it is passed and signed by the President, it becomes a law.
Bill of credit	A kind of paper money issued by the states before the Constitution was adopted. The Constitution prohibited states from issuing them so that only Congress would have the power to coin money and regulate its value.
Capital crime	An offense punishable by death.
Capitation tax	A tax put directly upon each person. It takes the same amount from everyone, rich and poor.
Cession	Giving up land to another government.
Commerce	Buying, selling, and transporting goods and services between places, such as states.
Common law	The body of laws that comes from court decisions of the past rather than from written laws. Common law was built up over centuries and represents our legal tradition. It extends back into British history.
Compulsory process	A court's power to order a person to appear in court to testify. In the Sixth Amendment, this power may be used to guarantee that witnesses will testify in behalf of an accused person. The order is called a subpoena (suh-pee-nah).
Concurrence	Agreement.
Confederation	A group of independent states or nations united for mutual advantages but without giving up power to act independently.
Constitute	To establish or bring into being.
Constitution	The fundamental law of an organized group. It establishes its government system and the principles guiding its operation.

Construed	Interpreted or understood to have a particular meaning.
Convene	To bring together a group for the purpose of conducting a meeting.
Corruption of blood	"Blood" here means members of a guilty person's family. Corruption of blood means making those family members share in the guilt.
Crime	An offense against society in violation of public law and punishable mainly by death, imprisonment, or fine.
Devolve	To pass authority to someone else. The authority to vote for president is passed to the House of Representatives.
Due process of law	The precautions which the government must take to protect the lives, liberty, and property of individuals when the government is dealing with them.
Duty	A tax on the value of goods shipped, most often, into a country.
Elector	One who has authority to elect someone to an official position—either a citizen in public elections or one who is authorized in the electoral system to cast a vote for president.
Emolument	A salary or fee.
Enumeration	A list of rights or powers.
Equity	Fairness. Settling a dispute which cannot be covered by written laws. Each party states its side, and the court makes a judgment based on what is most reasonable and just.
Ex post facto law	A law that makes something illegal and also provides punishment for those who did it before it was made illegal.
Excise	A tax upon certain products, such as leather goods or jewelry.

Executive	In government, the authority which carries out, or executes, the laws.
Felony	A serious crime that is punished by a longer term of imprisonment than a misdemeanor.
Full faith and credit	The recognition by each state of every other state's official proceedings. For example, one state recognizes the driver's license of an individual from another state as evidence that the person is a qualified driver.
Grand jury	A special jury that decides whether there is enough criminal evidence against a person to formally charge him or her in court.
Grievance	A complaint about something unjust that was done.
Habeas corpus	A court order requiring authorities to bring into writ of court a person being held by them. The court will set a deadline after which the prisoner must either be charged with an offense and scheduled for court appearance, or be set free.
Imminent	Threatening to happen very soon.
Immunities	Freedom from, or protection against, unjust government action. The First Amendment freedoms are immunities.
Impeachment	A formal accusation charging a government official with a crime or other serious wrongdoing.
Impost	A tax, especially one paid on goods entering the country.
Inauguration	The ceremony in which an individual is installed as president and receives the powers of the office.
Indictment	A formal accusation of a serious crime which is voted by a grand jury.

Infamous	Vicious, immoral, evil. A felony is an infamous crime.
Insurrection	Armed uprising against authority, but not as organized and widespread as rebellion.
Involuntary servitude	Forced labor, usually of prison inmates.
Jeopardy	Danger or risk.
Judicial	The function of judging cases that arise under the laws.
Jurisdiction	Authority. The kinds of subjects and geographic area over which an official body has authority to make decisions and take action.
Legislative	Having the function of making laws.
Maritime	See "Admiralty."
Marque and reprisal	Authorization to private shipowners to attack enemy vessels.
Militia	A body of private citizens organized, trained, and prepared to carry out military activities, but only when called into service by government authorities in emergencies.
Misdemeanor	A crime, less serious than a felony, that carries a shorter jail sentence, usually less than a year.
Naturalization	The legal process by which an immigrant gets the same rights as a natural-born citizen.
Nobility	A class of people with titles of rank, such as duke or baron, who formerly had special rights that the majority of people did not have.
Ordain	To give authority.
Overt	Open to view.
Petition	To make a formal request.

Prejudice	To unfairly influence the way a person thinks or feels about something.
Presentment	A charge or accusation.
Probable cause	Sufficient reason for investigators to believe that something or someone is in the place to be searched.
Pursuance	"In pursuance thereof" means "in following the rules of" the Constitution.
Pro tempore	A Latin phrase meaning "for the time being."
Quorum	The smallest number of members who must be present for a group to make official decisions.
Ratification	Approval.
Rebellion	Open, organized, widespread efforts to overthrow the government. A more serious threat than an insurrection.
Redress	To correct something that is unjust.
Reprieve	A delay or postponement.
Requisite	Required.
Revenue	Funds collected by government so that it may carry out its functions.
Securities	Stocks, which show a share of ownership in a business, or bonds, which show the amount of debt owed by a business or government to the holder or owner of the bond.
Service	"Held to service" means slavery.
Succeed	Taking over a position of authority after it has been vacated.
Suffrage	The right to vote.
Taxes	Required payments to government.
Tender	The way of making payment along with the material itself (gold, silver, bills, etc.)

Tonnage	A tax on boats based upon the number of tons of cargo they carry.
Treaty	An official agreement between two or more nations.
Tribunal	A court or other body which makes judgments.
Warrant	An authorization issued by a judge.
Writs of election	Orders to hold an election.
Yeas and nays	Yes and no votes.

822088